Helion & Company Limited
Unit 8 Amherst Business Centre
Budbrooke Road
Warwick
CV34 5WE
Tel 01926 499 619
Fax 0121 711 4075
email: info@helion.co.uk
website: www.helion.co.uk
Twitter: @helionbooks
Visit our blog http://blog.helion.co.uk

Published by Helion & Company 2018
Designed and typeset by Farr out Publications, Wokingham, Berkshire
Cover designed by Paul Hewitt, Battlefield Design (www.battlefield-design.co.uk)
Printed by Henry Ling Limited, Dorchester, Dorset

ISBN 978-1-912390-23-6

British Library Cataloguing-in-Publication Data
A catalogue record for this book is available from the British Library

For details of other military history titles published by Helion & Company Limited contact the above address, or visit our website: http://www.helion.co.uk

We always welcome receiving book proposals from prospective authors working in military history.

CONTENTS

INTRODUCTION

During 1932, the occupation of the Colombian towns of Leticia and Tarapacá, in the Amazon region, by Peruvian troops and civilians, led to a conflict that almost ended in a total war between the two countries. Aviation played an important role on both sides, due to the complicated jungle environment which made any land movement almost impossible. After some ground and air combats, a ceasefire was agreed, and the conflict was resolved. But the war over the Putumayo area became the baptism of fire of the Peruvian and Colombian air arms, leading, in the second case, to the development of their military aviation, which was almost non-existent in 1932. For Peru, the result of the conflict was also a rearming process, which proved important when, in 1941, they entered into war with Ecuador.

PART 1

FROM VICEROYALTIES TO REPUBLICS WITH UNCLEAR BORDERS

Chapter 1
PERU, THE ORIGINS OF A NEW REPUBLIC

The fall of the Inca Empire, occurring shortly after the arrival of the Spanish conquistadors, unleashed a conflict between the victorious forces, generated by the greed and private interests of these adventurers. On 20 November 1542 in Barcelona, in order to conclude these disputes and bring order to the newly conquered lands, King Carlos I of Spain signed, by means of Royal Decree, the so-called New Laws. These were a legislative assembly for the new territories – also known as the "Indies" – among them the creation of the Viceroyalty of Peru to replace the former governorships of Nueva Castilla and Nueva Leon. This process also arranged the transfer of the headquarters of the *Real Audiencia de Panama* to Lima, the so-called "City of Kings", capital of the new viceroyalty.

The new viceroyalty was an immense territory, which for more

Map of South America in 1750.

than two hundred years dominated much of South America, although Venezuela and Brazil, the latter belonging to Portugal and located on the shores of the Atlantic Ocean, remained outside its domain.

However, during the course of the eighteenth century the area of the viceroyalty suffered three major losses with the creation – from part of its territory – of two new viceroyalties of the Spanish crown: the Viceroyalty of New Granada and later the Viceroyalty of the Rio de la Plata, while, almost at the same time, the borders of Portugal were extended to the Amazon. Nevertheless, in spite of these losses, towards the beginning of the nineteenth century the *Virreinato del Peru* remained the main possession of the Spanish Crown, being one of its main sources of wealth.

It was with the process of Spanish-American independence that the end of the viceroyalty began, although it functioned as an important bastion and strategic centre of the Spanish crown in South America. As a result, war broke out with the Rio de la Plata, which had chosen the road to independence in 1810, sending liberating expeditions to the former territories of the viceroyalty. Thus, after achieving the independence of Chile, the general of the Rio de la Plata José de San Martín focused his attention on Peru. After landing successfully in the south of Lima and putting the royalist forces in retreat, San Martin declared the Republic of Peru, after which he retired from his military career. The work of ending the remnants of the royalist forces in Peru fell to General Simón Bolívar, a native of the Gran Colombia, who, with the support of the Peruvian guerrillas and all the logistics resources of the Andes Mountains, undertook a campaign with the purpose of definitively defeating the royalist forces. It was his decisive victory in the Battle of Ayacucho that left the forces of the old viceroyalty divided, debilitated and without possibility of being aided from the metropolis, causing its eventual disappearance in 1824, substituting in its place instead the Republic of Peru, which, although very diminished territorially, retained much of the old territory of the extinct viceroyalty.

Chapter 2
FROM NUEVA GRANADA TO COLOMBIA

Meanwhile, the Viceroyalty of Nueva Granada had its origins in 1508, when the so-called "*Tierra Firme*" was divided between Diego de Nicuesa, who obtained the governorship of Veragua or Castilla de Oro, which ran from the Atrato River, in the Gulf of Urabá, to Cape Gracias a Dios (current territories of Nicaragua, Costa Rica and Panamá), while Alonso de Ojeda obtained that of Nueva Andalusia, from the Atrato River to the end of Cabo de la Vela (almost the entire Caribbean coast of current Colombia). Shortly after, from 1 March 1511, Vasco Núñez de Balboa happened to take charge of Veragua, being named as lieutenant of the viceroy Diego Colón, in Darien. Shortly thereafter, on 23 December 1511, the king appointed him as captain and interim governor of the Darien until July 1514, this being a territory occupying the south of Panama and the northwest of Colombia. On 25 September 1513, he took possession of the "South Sea" he had discovered (the Pacific Ocean).

In May 1513 Pedrarias Dávila was appointed governor and captain general of Castilla de Oro, territory that included all the coast from the Cabo de la Vela to the territories that form the present Panama, with the exception of Veragua. After arriving in Darién in July 1514, Pedrarias Dávila founded the city of Nuestra Señora de la Asunción de Panamá on 15 August 1519. With the suppression of Nueva Andalucía, Balboa received, on 23 September 1514, the appointment of "*Gobernador de Coiba y Panamá y Adelantado de la Mar del Sur*", subordinate to Castilla de Oro.

In 1525, Fernandez de Oviedo attempted to establish a government in the area of Cartagena, called the Governorate of Cartagena, but did not prosper until the foundation of the city in 1533. On 26 February 1538, the *Real Audiencia de Panamá* was established in the Isthmus of Panamá by Royal Issue issued by King Carlos V. By 1542 there were the governorates of Santa Marta (founded in 1525), Cartagena and Popayán, the latter founded in 1536. In 1550, the *Real Audiencia Santafé de Bogotá* was created within the Viceroyalty of Peru, with jurisdiction over the *Nuevo Reino de Granada* and the governorates of Santa Marta, Cartagena and Popayán. In 1567, captain Andrés Gómez

Map showing the region of the Putumayo with the modus vivendi agreed between Colombia and Peru by 1905 (the black dashed line on the right shows the border). This was later changed by the Salomón – Lozano Treaty.

Hernández was appointed governor of the Governorate of Chocó, Dabaibe and Valle del Baeza, but never arrived at his destination as he died in Cartagena.

However, the weak dependence that existed between the government of the *Nuevo Reino de Granada at Santafé de Bogotá* and that of the Viceroyalty of Peru in Lima, caused largely by the slow communications between the two cities, as well as the constant conflicts between the government of the presidents of the *Real Audiencia of Santafé de Bogotá*, and the archbishopric of Santafé since 1582, led the court of Felipe V, in 1717, to establish an independent viceroyalty in Nueva Granada. This was provisionally erected on 13 June 1718, until the arrival of the first viceroy two years later, on 25 November 1719.

Two facts influenced the decision of the crown for the creation of this viceroyalty. First, that the area was an important centre of gold production and, secondly, its strategic location between the two oceans, serving as a gateway to the west of South America, and being strategically equipped to better deal with smuggling and pirate attacks from a point closer to the Caribbean.

However, the difficult and diverse geography of northern South America and the scarcity of appropriate roads once again caused the crown to seek greater efficiency in the administration of its territories. With the establishment of a general captaincy in Caracas and a royal audience in Quito, both legally subordinated to the viceroy, an attempt was made to respond to the needs of governing the most remote regions. In this way, the viceroyalty was formed by the *Nuevo Reino de Granada* (governorates of Nuevo Reino, Cartagena, Santa Marta, Maracaibo, Antioquia, Popayán and Guayana), Quito (governorates of Quito, Quijos, Macas, Esmeraldas and some corregimientos) and Panama (governorates of Panama and Veraguas). The governorates of Guayana, Margarita, Mérida and Maracaibo were later included in the *Capitanía General* (General Captaincy) *de Venezuela*. By 1764 the Government of Guayaquil was created, while on 13 February 1789, the province of Riohacha was separated from that of Santa Marta. Both had been fused on 17 January 1593.

The territories of the viceroyalty gained their independence from Spain between 1819 and 1822, after a series of military and political revolts, later unifying with those of the former *Capitanía General de Venezuela* to found the first Republic of Colombia, also known as Gran Colombia, the name with which it is remembered today. It was created in 1819 by the Congress gathered in the city of Angostura through the Fundamental Law of the Republic, later ratified at the Congress of Cúcuta in 1821, when the National Constitution was drafted and the country adopted the system of a republic with unitary centralism. The country was formed by the union of Venezuela and Nueva Granada in a single nation under the name of Republic of Colombia, later joined by Panama (1821) and Ecuador (1822). The term Gran Colombia is used in historiography to distinguish it from the present Republic of Colombia.

This republic existed juridically between 1821 and 1831 and was formed from the union of the former colonial entities of the Viceroyalty of Nueva Granada, the *Capitanía General de Venezuela*, the Presidency of Quito and the Free Province of Guayaquil. Its surface corresponded to the territories of the present republics of Colombia, Ecuador, Panama and Venezuela – including Guayana Esequiba, in dispute between Guayana and Venezuela – and other territories that passed to Brazil, Peru, Nicaragua, and Honduras, by international agreements concluded between these countries and the republics arising from the dissolution of Gran Colombia.

On the other hand, the international recognition of the legitimate existence of Gran Colombia, as an independent, sovereign and delimited territory, was part of a diplomatic context that in Europe was adverse to the formal recognition of the independence of the American countries. Thus, Austria, France, and Russia only recognized the independence of America if the new states submitted to a monarchical system by appointing members of the European dynasties as rulers. In addition, Colombia and the international powers faced different positions regarding the extension of the Colombian territory and its border delimitation.

At the time of its creation, Gran Colombia was the most prestigious Spanish-American country in the world, so much so that several politicians from Europe and America, including John Quincy Adams, then Secretary of State and future President of the United States, called it one of the most powerful nations of the planet. This prestige, added to the figure of Bolivar, attracted towards the nation Unionist ideas from independentist movements of Cuba, the Dominican Republic and Puerto Rico, that tried to form a state associated with the republic.

Eventually, Gran Colombia was dissolved in the late 1820s and early 1830s because of both the political differences that existed between supporters of federalism and centralism, and the regional tensions between the peoples that made up the republic, being created, after the dismemberment of its territory, the republics of Ecuador, Panama, Venezuela and Colombia. [1]

Chapter 3
THE BEGINNING OF THE CONFLICT

La Pedrera and the Salomón-Lozano Treaty

Since independence, the boundaries of all Latin American nations have been ambiguous, even more so in remote or inaccessible areas such as the Amazon. Thus, at the beginning of the twentieth century, while Colombia suffered the War of the Thousand Days, some Peruvian entrepreneurs, such as Casa Arana, based in Iquitos and dedicated to rubber extraction, entered the Amazonian territories between the Putumayo and Caquetá river basins. According to their claim, by right and according to the content of the Royal Decree of 1802, these areas corresponded to Peru. This caused the protest of the Colombian government, which denounced that the Peruvian government was militarizing the Putumayo, Napo and Caquetá rivers. The Peruvian occupation of the territories referred to had been practiced since 1896 by Casa Arana, and since 1900 by the Peruvian military, who opened a garrison that year in Tarapacá. Arana, with the support of the armed forces, evicted all the Colombian owners installed in the area, thus strengthening their monopoly position as the main producer and exporter of rubber throughout the region, and enslaving large numbers of indigenous people in the region to obtain cheap labour.

The Putumayo had slowly become a territory guarded by Peruvian troops and authorities, without the government of Colombia making a claim. Thus, in February 1911 the Peruvian government, led by Augusto B. Leguia, ordered his army to deploy troops in order to reinforce the Iquitos garrison. In this way, the No. 9 Battalion stationed in Chiclayo, on the north coast of Peru, was sent to the east under the command of Lieutenant Oscar Raimundo Benavides. The arrival of these Peruvian troops in the territory in dispute generated alarm in the Colombian citizenship: In the streets of Bogota the gravity of the events was denounced, predicting a second "Panama", this time at the hands of the Peruvians.

Thus, on 27 January 1911, the government of Carlos Eugenio Restrepo, in the face of the pressure of denunciations and the fear of revolt given the proximity of these events to the excision of Panama, sent a small force commanded by General Isaías Gamboa, of ten

Picture of Tarapacá before the conflict.

officers and NCOs and 47 soldiers, to make a presence on the right bank of the Caqueta River. These men, after sailing through the Atlantic Ocean, the Amazon and Caquetá Rivers, settled on 11 April in the base of La Pedrera, composed of a 6-kilometer trail, a plot of 3,000 square meters for crops and a set of trenches, where they created a permanent camp. However, the endemic diseases of the region soon took their toll, and many soldiers fell victim to malaria, yellow fever or Leishmaniasis. This situation was aggravated on 10 July 1911, when the Peruvian commander Óscar R. Benavides made a demonstration with his troops, demanding the withdrawal of Colombian forces. This was refused on 12 July, but not before a number of skirmishes that caused casualties on both sides. While the Colombian forces lost equipment and at least 15 men, among them General Gabriel Valencia, they claimed to have caused almost half a hundred casualties to the attackers. The Peruvians, on the other hand, were victims of a ferocious Beri-Beri epidemic and Yellow Fever, which resulted in casualties averaging 30 men a day. Unable to maintain the operational rhythm in these conditions, Benavides ordered the withdrawal of his forces on 16 October and by 6 November, the incident was declared over, normalizing relations between Colombia and Peru. Following this incident, the governments of Colombia and Peru arranged the demilitarization of the area, generating a Modus Vivendi that would create problems in the future.

A decade later, on 24 March 1922, Augusto B. Leguia was back in office and, with the intention of settling the border dispute with Colombia, authorized the signature of the so called Salomon-Lozano Treaty[2], by which Peru granted Colombia sovereignty over the territories between the Caquetá and Putumayo rivers, as well as an adjacent territorial fringe – known as the Amazon Trapeze – which gave Colombia its long-sought access to the Amazon River, this in exchange for Colombian recognition of Peruvian sovereignty over the previously disputed territories south of the Putumayo and the transfer of a territorial fringe denominated "*Triangulo de Sucumbios*", a small but strategically important territory located between the Putumayo and San Miguel rivers in the north-western corner of the Amazon rain forest. What may have seemed strange to many Peruvians – perhaps because of the conspicuous silence kept by Leguía's political enemies regarding this matter – was the fact that such a territorial exchange allowed Peru to "block" Ecuador in its pretensions towards the Amazon, and would eventually allow for the signature of agreements favourable to Peruvian interests. Consequently, the territorial cessions gave Colombia a harbour and free navigation on the Amazon, whilst Peru obtained a strategic victory in its quest to finalize the demarcation of the north and north-eastern borders. More importantly, the treaty pleased the United States Government, which was interested in compensating Colombia after its loss of Panama. Leguía, who was well-liked by the Americans, was able to secure US support for the upcoming negotiations for the return to national sovereignty of the former Peruvian territories of Tacna, Arica and Tarata. The treaty was ratified by both governments after the signature, on 4 March 1925 in Washington DC, of the Tripartite Act, between Colombia, Peru and Brazil, the later related to the line between the rivers Apaporis and Tabatinga that marked the Brazilian border with the disputed area.

After that, the borders were marked and, on 31 July 1930, Colombian Colonel Luis Acevedo received from the Peruvian Colonel T. Molina Darteano, head of the Loreto Department of Peru, the Amazonic Trapeze, signing an act on board of the Peruvian vessel *América* at Leticia.

The *Caucheros'* lack of vision and their refusal to give priority to national interests over their own made them fierce Treaty opponents and, in consequence, used their economic power to buy consciences and newspaper front pages in Lima, they accused Leguia's administration of treason, looking to erode the President's image – an offense that persists even today.

The occupation of Leticia

On 22 August 1930, Leguia's enemies finally secured their victory as the President was deposed by a *coup d'état* led by General Manuel Maria Ponce Brousset, himself later replaced by Colonel Luis Miguel Sanchez Cerro, who actually began the uprising against the government south of the country in the first place. Imprisoned and with his public image greatly tarnished, Leguía would become the only Peruvian Head of State to die in prison, passing away on 6 February 1932. The military *Junta de Gobierno* called for elections to be held in 1931; these were won by a thin margin by the *Unión Revolucionaria*, led by none other than Sanchez Cerro himself, who became president on 8 December 1931. His administration, heavily influenced by fascism, was marked by social convulsion stirred up by his enemies of the *Partido Comunista* (Communist Party, PC) and the *Alianza Popular Revolucionaria Americana* (American Popular Revolutionary Alliance, APRA)[3], whose violent uprisings forced the Government to deploy the Armed Forces in order to suppress their activities throughout the country.

It was during this difficult period, that, at dawn on 1 September 1932, a mixed group of 48 civilians and military elements, armed with 44 Winchester rifles and one revolver and acting under orders of the secretly organized *Junta Patriótica* (Patriotic Coalition Junta), mobilized from Iquitos towards the Colombian town of Leticia, located in the south-eastern corner of the so-called *Trapecio Amazonico*, and took it by surprise "in the name of the Peruvian people". They expelled the Colombian authorities, as well as the small Colombian Army garrison guarding Leticia, to the neighbouring Brazilian town of Benjamin Constant, where Alfredo Villamil Fajardo, the major of the Amazonas National Intendancy of Colombia, denounced what had happened.

Shortly afterwards, a group of the Peruvian forces went even further and also successfully occupied the town of Tarapacá, located at the upper right corner of the Trapeze, without bloodshed. After securing both places, the Junta ordered its agents and supporters in Lima to use the press to spread the false rumour that APRA was the political force backing them, in a risky gamble to secure the intervention of the Peruvian Government – a fierce APRA enemy – in its favour. An enraged Sanchez Cerro, unwilling to give his political enemies a single favourable point in the eyes of the public, decided to support the Junta's "spontaneous patriotic act" and, ignoring the Colombian call for an internal police-type solution, ordered an army mobilization on 6 September 1932. Neither Peru nor Colombia were ready militarily to face an international conflict, and despite Peru having a slight numerical advantage in terms of aircraft availability, it soon became clear that both countries would have to make substantial purchases in order to face the new situation. In the Peruvian case, it is very likely that the decision to confront Colombia was the result of a very superficial analysis of Colombian capabilities. The "*Plan de Guerra*" (War Plan) drawn up by the *Ejército del Perú* (or Peruvian Army –EP) high command included the following objectives:

- Primary objective: the control of the Putumayo River, considered an absolute priority, even more important than Leticia itself.
- Secondary objective: the capture and possession of the Caquetá River as an international border.

Simultaneously, the *Marina de Guerra del Perú* (or Peruvian Navy-MGP) began the planning of a blockade of the Colombian Pacific Ocean ports with the aim of cutting the Colombian shipping lanes, and thereby hoping to accelerate a ceasefire on favourable terms[4].

Meanwhile, in the Colombian capital Bogotá, the Peruvian decision provoked a furious reaction by President Enrique Olaya Herrera's administration, which had been waiting for a peaceful solution to the incident. Therefore, after taking notice of the belligerent Peruvian attitude, President Olaya called up the reserves and – to the Peruvians' surprise – appealed immediately for a massive international credit to purchase weapons required to equip a military expedition tasked with expelling the invaders from Colombian territory.

PART 2
CONTENDING SIDES

Chapter 4
THE AVIACIÓN MILITAR COLOMBIANA

The first step in the creation of the Colombian Military Aviation took place on 17 September 1916, when the Colombian president, José Vicente Concha, sanctioned the Law 15 to send a commission to foreign countries for training and to research new weapon technologies, including aviation, and when they returned to the country they must serve in the Army to create an aviation school. The war in Europe and other problems made this impossible and on 31 December 1919 the Law 126 was issued by president Marco Fidel Suárez, creating the *Escuela de Aviación Militar* (Military Aviation School) and added aviation as the fifth arm of the Army. This law was regulated by Decree 2172 of 10 December 1920.

The new school was built on part of the ground of the San Luis farm at Flandes, on the south bank of the Magdalena river, near the town of Girardot, about 100 kilometres to the southwest of Bogotá. The town was chosen for being close to the country's capital, at low altitude, and also close to the river that linked the capital with the Caribbean coast. Three Caudron G.3 (serials A-1 to A-3), three Caudron G.4 (A-4 to A-6) and four Nieuport Delage 11 Bebe (A-7 to A-10) were purchased, along with a French mission that was contracted to train the new crews. Instruction began on 15 February 1921.

Nine officers started the course, and on 18 June Major Félix Castillo made the first solo flight. Unfortunately, only one course graduated from the school, with five pilots, as the school was closed on 28 April 1922 when the French mission left the country. Two Caudron G.4 and one G.3 had been lost in accidents and the others were stored at Madrid Town, closer to Bogotá.

On 8 November 1924, president Pedro Nel Ospina issued decree 1756 to create the Base Arsenal Madrid and re-establish the school, but new planes needed to be bought as the others were in very bad condition and were obsolete.

On 10 September 1924, a Swiss mission arrived in Colombia to organize the new school, and along with them was one Swiss built Wild WT34D, with which the activities of the new school began on 15 February 1925. One month later, it was decided to buy three extra planes, but, in the meantime, the Caudron G.3 serialled A-1 was repaired and used briefly. The three new WT34D built by Comte arrived on November 1926, having some modifications to improve

The Caudron G-3 serialled A-1 was one of the first planes of the Military Aviation School of Flandes. Archive Santiago Rivas.

One of the four Nieuport Delage 11 Bebe used by the school of Flandes. Archive Santiago Rivas.

their performance in the conditions of Madrid, which was at about 2,600 meters over sea level, and the four examples were serialled 11 to 14. The first two were received on 12 January 1927 and the third on 8 February. Unfortunately, on 2 February 1927, the plane serial 11 had an accident and was repaired, but on 19 February the plane serial 12 was destroyed in another accident.

It was also decided to buy five planes for advanced training and light attack from the same constructor, but built by Comte in France, named Wild-Comte X, and were requested with 550 hp Gnome Rhone Jupiter engines instead of the projected 450 hp Lorraine Dietrich. This order was later increased to eight examples. They received serials 101 to 108 and had two machine guns for the observer in the rear seat, and one on the nose, being the first armed planes of the force. They arrived from May to November 1928, but the plane 108 was sent directly to New York to be used by aviator Camilo Daza in a flight to Colombia, which failed. The plane was sent to Colombia to be rebuilt.

On 23 November 1928 Captain Méndez Rey, together with US pilot John Tod-Hunter, who was contracted to provide training after the Swiss mission left the country, made the first flight from the USA to Colombia in a Curtiss Falcon with pontoons, baptized "Ricaurte", flying from New York to Madrid with stops at Jacksonville, La Habana (Cuba), Puerto Barrios (Guatemala), Puerto Cabezas (Nicaragua), Colón (Panama), Barranquilla and Girardot.

The last two Wild W34D (serials 11 and 14) were retired by 1930, so new basic trainers were purchased in 1931, being ten Curtiss J 2 Fledgling, with the first three received on November of that year with serials B-101 to 103, and changed to serials 15 to 17. The others, with serials up to 24, were received between 1932 and 1933. Also, by the end of 1931, three Curtiss CW-14R Osprey were purchased and delivered to Cali by the beginning of 1932, with serials 301 to 303 – later changed to 121 to 123 – but they were still disassembled when the conflict with Peru erupted.

As of 1 September, 1932, the *Aviación Militar Colombiana* was still a very small force comprising only the small aviation school, and equipped with a handful of aircraft, none of which had substantial military capabilities, including:

- 1 Curtiss D-12 Falcon (named Ricaurte)
- 7 Wild-Comte X (serials 101 to 106 and 108)
- 3 Curtiss J-2 Fledgling (serials 15 to 17).

Wild-Comte X planes at a hangar at Madrid airfield, where the Military Aviation School was moved after serving briefly at Flandes. Photo Gumersindo Cuellar.

The Curtiss D-12 Falcon baptized "Ricaurte" was the only fighter aircraft of the Colombian military aviation when the conflict started, but had no weapons and saw no combat. Photo Gumersindo Cuellar.

From the above list, only the D-12 Falcon and the Wild-Comte X had any kind of offensive capabilities, but the "Ricaurte" wasn't armed. The Fledglings had a single Browning machine gun, used for training. Their limited numbers and short operational range, however, were reason enough for the Colombian Government to urgently consider launching a rearming process.

The role of SCADTA

It is very important to understand the role played by *Sociedad Colombo-Alemana de Transportes Aereos* (German-Colombian Aerial Transport Company, SCADTA), the main airline operating in Colombia at the time, in the development of the activities of the *Aviación Militar de Colombia* over the Putumayo. Established at the end of 1919 by German immigrants, this company possessed, by late 1932, a relatively modern fleet of aircraft as well as an elaborate support infrastructure for operations and, perhaps more importantly, crews familiar with aerial navigation over long distances in the Colombian environment.

Once the Leticia incident was known, the Colombian Minister of War, Captain Carlos Uribe Gaviria, invited the company's representative in the Colombian capital, Herman Kuehl, to the premises of the Ministry of Foreign Affairs in order to study a map showing the difficult situation facing his country. Next to Kuehl was also the German citizen Herbert Boy, the company's most experienced pilot at the time, with the intention of arranging his incorporation into the Military Aviation. To do this, Boy left the ranks of SCADTA and was incorporated into the Colombian Military Aviation as "technical adviser" with the honorary rank of major, and a monthly salary allowance of 600 Pesos[5].

Aware of the reality of the human and material shortcomings that afflicted the Military Aviation, the Colombian government negotiated the inclusion of personnel in the service of SCADTA to the ranks of the Military Aviation in order that these experienced aviators take

View of the Curtiss Falcon "Ricaurte". The plane was lost shortly after the conflict ended and was never found. Photo Gumersindo Cuellar.

The "Ricaurte" at Madrid airfield. Photo Gumersindo Cuellar.

part in the military operations planned against the Peruvian forces. Thus, by Decree No. 1543 dated 23 September 1932, the President of Colombia, Enrique Olaya Herrera, in the exercise of his legislative powers, ordered:

1) The creation of the following positions, with their corresponding ranks, in the *Flotilla Aérea de Guerra Amazónica* (Amazon War Air Flotilla):

A pilot, a mechanic in chief and two mechanics, positions that fell to the German citizens Hans Werner von Engel, with the rank of Captain; Alfred Welfert, Simon Butz, Helmut Roesel, with the rank of First Sergeants. These men were assigned with the positions of pilot, mechanic in chief and mechanics, enjoying a salary of 500, 450 and 250 pesos, respectively.

2) In addition, by Decree No. 1615 of 30 September of that same year, a pilot position was created at the Military Aviation School for the Colombian citizen José Ignacio Forero, who was awarded the rank of Captain and a monthly remuneration of 126 pesos.

3) Finally, it is necessary to indicate that, in anticipation of the actions taken by the Peruvians, the Military Aviation of Colombia, on 3 August 1932, established the rules of admission for the postulants, all from the Colombian Army, to the School of Military Aviation. The selected officers would go on to offer services in commission within the Aviation School where they would take the course of flights, complemented with an observation, to opt, if they approve, for the diploma of Military Pilot and to become part, definitively, of the Aviation arm.[6]

The facts detailed above would be of enormous importance in the development of the activities of the Military Aviation over the Putumayo. Thanks to the inclusion of the pilots, mechanics and infrastructure of SCADTA, as well as the use of its network of contacts for the acquisition of spare parts and aircraft, the *Aviación Militar Colombiana* was able to make its expansion process more flexible.

After the agreements with SCADTA, the structure of the *Aviación Militar Colombiana* was established as follows:

1. Command and personnel

- General Alfredo Vasquez Cobo, Chief of the Colombian Amazon Military Expedition.

The Curtiss Fledglings serialled 15 and 16 with a pilot with flight equipment. They were extensively used for liaison from Madrid with the airfields to the south of Colombia.

One of the three Curtiss Fledglings of the Aviación Militar Colombiana. Archive Santiago Rivas.

The three Curtiss Fledglings of the Aviación Militar Colombiana. Photo Gumersindo Cuellar.

- Mayor Herbert Boy, Technical advisor.
- 53 pilots, from the school and SCADTA. These were then reinforced by a further group of 17 pilots from SCADTA – as part of the agreement between SCADTA and the Colombian Military Aviation – under which the former provided both flight and ground personnel that operated the services of the later, in order to fill their gaps in that field. Although this list consisted mostly of German citizens, it also included, albeit to a lesser extent, pilots from Italy and the US. These men, along with the ranks assigned to them as part of the *Aviación Militar Colombiana*, are detailed below:

The "Bucaramanga" was the ninth F13 of SCADTA, received in 1925. It was later transferred to the Air Arm. Archive Mauricio Umaña.

Name	Nationality	Rank
Herbert Boy	German	Colonel
Fritz Von Donop	German	Captain
F. Tessen Von Heydebreck	German	Captain
Karl Maringer	German	Captain
Von Oertzen	German	Captain
Helmut Roeder	German	Captain
Hans Wermer Von Engel	German	Captain
Olaf Bielenstein	German	Captain
Ferruccio Guicciardi	Italian	Captain
Hans Kindermann	German	Captain
Alexander Mauke	German	Captain
Johan Risticz	German	Captain
Rudolf Starke	German	Captain
Ludwig Graf Schaesberg	German	Captain
Henry Grautoff	German	Captain
Hans Dietrich Hoffman	German	Captain
Helmuth Koening	German	Lieutenant

2. Air bases

- Guabito, located in Cali, home of the *Escuela de Aviación Militar* (Military Aviation School) "Marco Fidel Suárez". Inaugurated in 1933, when it was moved from Madrid to the new location, with better facilities.
- Flandes, located near the city of Girardot, about 100km south west of Bogota on the banks of the Magdalena River. This was the location of the headquarters of operations of SCADTA.
- Mayor Justo Mariño Air Base, in Madrid.
- Palanquero Air Base, in the Cundinamarca region, built up during the war from the basis of the SCADTA base there. The airfield, built by SCADTA on land belonging to Mr. Ruperto Aya and Mr. Diógenes Troncoso, was purchased by the government.
- Caucayá auxiliary airfield.
- Tres Esquinas auxiliary base on the Caquetá.
- Potosí auxiliary base.
- Puerto Arica auxiliary base.
- Puerto Boy auxiliary base in Curiplaya.

Following its inclusion in the Military Aviation structure, the Flandes base, the main base of SCADTA located on the banks of the Magdalena River, quickly became the training centre for the military personnel coming from Guabito Aviation School in Cali. In this

The C-25 "Boyacá", which was the second F13fe of SCADTA with new rudder and balanced rudder and elevators. The BMW IV engine with two blade propeller was later replaced by a BMW V with three blade one. Archive R.E.G. Davies.

The sole Junkers W33 of SCADTA, baptized "Cundinamarca", used for photo survey missions and transferred to the Air Arm. Archive Santiago Rivas.

The "Cúcuta" of Cosada airline, a subsidiary of SCADTA, after receiving the BMW Va engine of 360hp and the new serial C-38. Archive Mauricio Umaña.

The Wal C-28 "Colombia" was the third and last Wal received by the airline and was transferred to the Military Aviation in 1932. Archive Santiago Rivas

The Merkur C-27 "Pedro Nel Ospina" at Girardot. Archive Mauricio Umaña.

The C-25 was delivered to the Colombian Air Arm during the conflict with Peru and received the serial 203. It was later re-serialled PF-2. Archive Santiago Rivas.

location, the training flights of the military personnel coming from Guabito were continued, using the Comte-Wild Xs serialled 105 and 108, as well as one Junkers W33 and two F13s of SCADTA, with the purpose of instructing the crews in amphibious and offensive operations, and thus enable them safely to operate the combat aircraft whose acquisition was being managed by the Colombian government. Meanwhile, in Madrid instruction in gunnery, navigation and bombing were resumed, using the Curtiss Fledgling that had been adapted for that purpose.

In addition, tests were also carried out at Madrid of demolition bombs manufactured by the company Jaramillo y Co., located in Bogotá, using the Curtis Fledgling serial 17. Only seven of the sixteen bombs dropped during these tests exploded, because the fulminant was installed wrongly, but it was decided to deploy them anyway. The Fledglings were also used to train the crews on the use of the machine guns.

In an agreement between SCADTA and the government, the Junkers F13 serials C-21 named "Bucaramanga", C-25 "Boyacá" and C-38 "Cúcuta", the Dornier Merkur C-27 "Pedro Nel Ospina", the Junkers W33 C-33 "Cundinamarca", the Fokker Super Universal C-44 "Medellín", and the Dornier Wal "Colombia" were sold and started to serve on transport and reconnaissance duties, being the first transports of the Military Aviation. The F13s were re-serialled 201 to 203 (later the 201 and 203 received serials PF-1 and PF-2, PF of Policía Fronteriza, Border Police), the Wal became 601, the Merkur 602, the W33 became 204, and the Super Universal 205. The W33 received a dorsal gunner's position in an opening on the roof, with a

The F13 203 of the Colombian Air Arm seen after the conflict with Peru. Archive Javier Franco.

One of the three K43 built for Colombia, during tests in Sweden before delivery. Archive Lennart Andersson.

twin machine gun mounting in the opening for the load hatch.

All of these machines, except the F13s, were of recent manufacture or were in good operational condition. In addition, the Colombian Government made good use of the company's elaborate supply system, allowing easier acquisition of aircraft and supplies worldwide, thus accelerating the Military Aviation process of expansion.

Besides the planes of SCADTA, a single Hamilton H-45 light transport was purchased by Andian National Corp., an oil company operating in Colombia, which was baptized "Águila II" by the company, and serialled 205.

One of the three Colombian K43 at AB Flygindustri in Sweden before delivery. Archive Lennart Andersson.

Ju52/3m serialled 622 together with a K43 at Palanquero Air Base on the Magdalena River. Archive Javier Franco.

Rearming: The Defence Collection

With the social and economic support of the population, the Colombian government launched a massive military rearming process and announced the imminent deployment of a military expedition to the Putumayo River with the objective of re-establishing control over Leticia and Tarapacá.

Since it was unable to divert funds immediately for the purchase of new equipment, the Colombian government called for civilian support in the form of a national "Defence Collection" promptly organized with the aim to raise the required funds for the immediate purchase of aircraft and other military equipment while, almost simultaneously, the Congress passed a law authorizing the State's external indebtedness for the purchase of weaponry. The patriotic fervour woke up Colombian society, and in a short time the initiative was able to raise more than $10 million dollars[7], funds which were quickly invested in the purchase of aircraft and other equipment.

Meanwhile, Wilhelm Schnurbusch from SCADTA was commissioned by the Colombian government to go to Europe to buy some of the planes, purchasing a batch of three Junkers K43do, six W34[8], six Ju52/3m[9], two Dornier Do C 2A two seat fighters (serialled 851 and 852) and two extra Wals[10] of the military version, all arriving from the beginning of 1933. Together with the new German planes, a German Aeronautical Mission was contracted to train the Colombian crews, and their five pilots took part in the war.

Three of the Ju52/3m were being negotiated for SCADTA, but the company transferred the negotiation to the Colombian government. Initially the Colombian government ordered twelve, but the Germans only agreed to sell the original three due to their own needs, but later allowed the sale of another three planes. The first three planes were originally started as single-engined Ju52, and were modified on the

The Ju52/3m serialled 621 at Bogotá. Archive Javier Franco.

Another view of the 621, flying and equipped with floats. Archive Javier Franco.

Two Ju52/3m equipped with floats and with their dorsal positions seen at Palanquero. One if the 622 and the other is 625 or 626. Archive Javier Franco.

The plane serialled 622. The first three planes had a different windscreen from the later ones, which received the later windscreen used in most Ju52/3m. Archive Javier Franco.

The plane 625 in the thirties. Note the windscreen is different from that on the planes 621 to 623 and has the original engine cowlings. Photo Gumersindo Cuellar.

Interesting picture of a Colombian Air Arm Ju52/3m with the two dorsal positions for machine guns and the ventral one, all equipped with their weapons. Archive Javier Franco.

production line to three-engined Ju52/3m. They were the third to fifth three-engined Ju52s built (the first two were sent to Bolivia). They also had the original type of windscreen used on the first Ju52. Also, the W34s were part of a batch of four purchased for SCADTA and were ready to be shipped. The fourth plane of that batch was delivered to

One of the two Dornier Do C2A delivered to the Colombian Air Arm during the conflict with Peru, despite which it wasn't used on war missions. Archive Günther Ott.

View of Palanquero air base in times of the conflict.

One of the two Consolidated P2Y-1C at Cartagena. Even though the planes were received with camouflage, they were sent to Buenaventura to operate over the Pacific Ocean.

the airline, with the serial C-49 and baptized "Cundinamarca", arriving with the airline on 7 January 1933. The three W34s were sent to AB Flygindustri in Sweden, where they were modified with bomb racks and gunner positions with Madsen 7.9mm machine guns, receiving the designation K43do and equipped with Pratt & Whitney Wasp S3H1 engines. They received a mottled camouflage, used in their first years of service.

It is interesting to note that the Do C 2As were the unique examples of the model built. The first was as Do C 3, being a reconnaissance and attack three-seat sesquiplane based on the Do 10, and first flew on 18 September 1931 with an Hispano Suiza engine of 625hp. This plane was later converted into a high wing monoplane with a Hispano Suiza 12 NBr engine of 740hp and an extra fuel tank behind the engine, in place of one of the seats, and was named Do C 2A. A second example was built and both were delivered to Colombia.

Meanwhile, another commission of the Colombian Military Aviation went to the United States and purchased thirty Curtiss Model 35A Hawk II[11] fighters (serials 801 to 830), two Consolidated P2Y-1C[12] flying boats for patrol and bombing (serials 610 and 611), and 20 Curtiss Model 37F Cyclone Falcon[13] for attack (serialled 111 to 130), followed later by another order for five Cyclone Falcon to replace lost examples, receiving serials 111A, 115A, 116A, 118A and 131.

Most of the aircraft listed above arrived in Colombian territory in time to take part in military actions, with the exception of 18 of the Hawk IIs and the second batch of five Cyclone Falcons, for whose orders – due to their numbers – were only partially fulfilled by the time of the cease-fire of May 1933.

Chapter 5
THE CUERPO DE AVIACIÓN DEL PERÚ

Historical Background

The history of military aviation in Peru began on the morning of 2 December 1915, when Captain Juan E. O'Connor of the *Ejército del Perú* (Peruvian Army, EP) took off from a small airfield located at Bellavista, near the port of Callao, aboard a Bleriot XI with the aim of performing a tactical observation of the military manoeuvres scheduled during that day outside the city of Lima. This flight, unprecedented in Peruvian military history, marked the first use of aviation by Peruvian armed forces.

After completing his flight, O'Connor issued a thorough report to his superiors, detailing his impressions and recommendations for the future employment of aviation. Consequently, the High Command of the Armed Forces authorized preliminary studies for the creation of the Peruvian Army Aviation component, which were completed by mid-1916. It is worth pointing out that the Bleriot XI employed by O'Connor, acquired by the Army from local aviator José Montero, has to be considered to be – for all practical purposes – the first Peruvian military aircraft.

In June of 1916, and with the aim to form a core of competent aviators, the EP decided to send two of its more outstanding officers on an instructional tour to El Palomar military aviation school located in Buenos Aires, Argentina. However, after long bureaucratic delays that held them in town, Lieutenants Enrique Ruiz Espinoza and Guillermo Protzel del Castillo arrived in Buenos Aires at the beginning of 1918,

Boeing and Keystone aircraft from the Primera Escuadrilla de Reconocimiento seen parked at San Ramon airfield in the early thirties. Archive Instituto de Estudios Historico Aeroespaciales del Peru.

Rare view of the two Chance-Vought UO-1A used by the CAP on the shore at Paracas, near Pisco, 275 km to the south of Lima. The planes, initially painted in yellow, on the picture are wearing the new dark grey scheme introduced from July 1930. Archive IEHAP.

A nice side view of Boeing model 40B-2 assigned with the serial I-R-9. This particular machine flew passenger and cargo transport missions between Lima, San Ramon and Masisea. Archive IEHAP.

commencing their training immediately. Regrettably, shortly after the beginning of their training Lt. Ruiz Espinoza was killed in a flight accident when, at 1700 hrs on 13 May 1918, the Bleriot XI monoplane he was flying crashed at El Palomar airfield in Argentina. Far from being discouraged by this tragedy, his partners, Lt. Guillermo Protzel del Castillo and Peruvian civilians Mr. Enrique Parodi and Manuel Sanchez, whom had managed to arrive at El Palomar shortly after with their own funds, successfully managed to complete their flight training and returned to Perú by mid-November of that year. With them also arrived a Henri Farman biplane, a donation from the Peruvian residents in the city of Buenos Aires, which was christened as Teniente Ruiz in honour of the fallen Peruvian Aviator. In January 1919, Lt. Protzel employed this aircraft to continue flights in Perú and was followed shortly thereafter by the Midshipman Ismael Montoya, who in July 1919 also graduated from El Palomar flight school.

The Army Aviation Service

The Peruvian military aviation service was officially born with the issue of a Supreme Decree issued by President Jose Luis Pardo y Barreda, dated from January 28, 1919 which created the Servicio de Aviación del Ejército (Army Aviation Service, SAE) under the following guidelines:

THE PRESIDENT OF THE REPUBLIC, considering:
1º. – That an Army Aviation Service will constitute an indispensable institutional entity for the national defence;
2º. – That, at the time it is not possible to organize this service as autonomous entity, but only as a branch of the army;
3º. – Therefore, it is a requirement for the future organization of the service to train the personnel which would serve as the foundations for its definitive organization; and,
4º. – Having reviewed the project prepared by the Army´s Engineer Corps Direction:
DECREES:
Art.1º. – To create the "Servicio de Aviación del Ejército", which should: a) perform the study, acquisition and maintenance of aeronautical machines; b) administrate, instruct and mobilize all personnel linked to the service of such machines.
Art.2º. – At the time, the only operational section will be the Centro de Aviación (Aviation Centre), to be located in Lima, with the aim to create similar units within each military region.
Art.3º. – Each "Centro de Aviación" will act as a training school for future aviators and will provide, in the event of mobilization, air units or squadrons.
Art.4º – Each Air Squadron shall comprise:
a) Material. – 4 or 6 aircraft organized in two or three sections; a ground support unit with a number of indispensable vehicles allowing optimal operation of the unit (tractors, truck-shops and automobiles for liaison duties, wireless telegraph, etc.).
b) Personnel. – An aviation company whose composition will be established separately.
Art.5º. – Once established, all centres will become dependent of the Alta Dirección de Aeronáutica (High Aeronautic Bureau, ADA) comprising a High Command and a General Staff, with several units under their command including the maintenance station, on the front line.
Published in Lima on January 28, 1919.
Signed: José Pardo y Barreda José Juan Manuel Zuloaga

Following its foundation, the SAE initially operated from the Bellavista airfield, operating a mixture of French and British types

Ancón, mid-1933. A Chance-Vought UO-1A is hoisted on board the BAP *Almirante Grau* of the *Marina de Guerra del Perú* anchored at Ancón Bay, home of the *III Escuadrón de Aviación*. Archive Gonzalo Maguiña.

A rare view of Chance-Vought UO-1A Corsair serial A-P I-E-4 seen after being embarked aboard the cruiser BAP *Grau*. As this ship was not fitted with a catapult the aircraft had to be lowered to the water surface with the aid of a crane in order to deploy. Archivo Historico de la Marina.

Twelve Vought O2U-1E Corsair reconnaissance and light attack biplanes were purchased by the Peruvian government in July of 1930. By 1 September 1932 attrition and accidents had reduced the operational aircraft numbers to eight. Archive Instituto de Estudios Historico Aeroespaciales.

The Chance-Vought Corporation, a part of the United Aircraft and Transport Corporation, built the O2U Corsair series from 1927 to 1933 supplying aircraft to twelve operators across the globe, including Peru who purchased 12 units in July of 1930.

2nd Lt. Francisco Secada Vigneta stands in front of O2U-1E "Corsair" serial 5-E-6 shortly before leaving Las Palmas bound for the conflict area. Note the unusual Peruvian national identification stripes on the tail, product of a misinterpretation of instructions by the Chance-Vought corporation personnel. Archive IEHAP.

CAP personnel stand in front of a Vought Corsair parked at San Ramón airfield during the *8th Escadrille* mobilization to the conflict area. Note the presence of the engine speed ring, seldom seen on Peruvian Corsairs. Archive Humberto Currarino.

such as the Avro 504K, Caudron G.3, Salmson 2A.2 and Bristol F.2b. Shortly thereafter, in May 1929, operations were moved to Maranga airfield, were the *Centro de Aviación Militar* was established. By 1922, however, Maranga airfield proved to be too small to sustain the increased pace of operations and the Army sought a new location for its operations. This was finally found in the field of a large state farm, located south of Lima, known as Las Palmas. In July 1922, Las Palmas aerodrome was finally opened and became the home of the newly established *Escuela Central de Aviación Militar*.

The Naval Aviation Corps

Shortly after the creation of the Army Aviation, the *Marina de Guerra del Perú* (Peruvian Navy, MGP) – also got its own aviation service with the issuing of a Supreme Decree dated 26 January 1920; this created the *Cuerpo de Aviación Naval* (Naval Aviation Corps, CAN), which was put under the command of Capitan de Fragata Juan Leguia Swayne, president Leguia´s own son. First operating from a small base in the San Lorenzo Island, near Lima, the CAN operations were

Sotziki, late November of 1932. Members of the Ashaninka tribe provide the CAP personnel with assistance in the conversion to floats of Corsair serial 2-E-3. This particular aircraft had just left the workshop as evidenced by the repainted tail national colours. Archive IEHAP.

Members of the local population of Sotziki, composed mostly by Ashaninka tribe members and migrants from the capital city, gather around Vought 2-E-4 during the conversion works in November of 1932.

Sotziki, November of 1932. Archaic but effective, a pulley was employed to raise the aircraft while floats were fitted in place. Note the erroneous style of Peruvian markings applied on the tail by Vought factory personnel, which were only removed in late 1932 as the aircraft headed to the front. Archive IEHAP.

Captain Leonardo Alvariño Herr pose next to his aircraft in this portrait taken shortly before his departure to the theatre of operations. Alvariño and his gunner disappeared without trace on March 22, 1933 while performing a dangerous liaison mission. Archive IEHAP.

soon moved to the Ancón Bay, located about 30 miles north of Lima, where a seaplane base and a training centre for naval aviators were established. Among the first aircraft assigned to the new-born service were a pair of Norman-Thompson NT-2B, six Curtiss model F Seagull and a trio of Georges-Levy GL.40B.2. After the reorganization of the naval services the CAN was put under the command of Harold B.Grow, an experienced United States Navy officer, and reequipped with new flying material including five Boeing model 21 trainers, five Curtiss H2L flying boats, four Douglas DT-2B bombers and a pair of Change-Vought OU-1A Corsair observation biplanes.

Unification of the Aviation Services: Birth of the Cuerpo de Aviación del Perú

During its first years of existence, both air services were reinforced with the arrival of several foreign military missions that took charge of the training, administration and, invariably, the re-equipment of these new forces and their elements. In the SAE's case, the French and

The only offensive Peruvian aircraft acquisitions to arrive in time to take part in the military operations were a handful of Douglas O-38P reconnaissance and light attack biplanes and Curtiss model 35A Hawk II, both powered by the same 640hp Wright R-1820F Cyclone engine. Archive Dan Hagedorn.

2nd Lt. Secada next to Vought serial 5-E-6 at San Ramon shortly before its departure towards Sotziki as part of the CAP deployment to the Amazon. Archive Humberto Currarino.

Ancón, February of 1933. Crew and ground personnel perform the last minute arrangements next to the Douglas ½-VG-3 and ½-VG-6. Shortly after, these aircraft left Ancón bound to the operations zone. Archive Dan Hagedorn.

British were briefly followed by the Germans who, with their missions composed of experienced airmen, prepared the path followed by the first promotions of local airmen, as well as preparing the organization and doctrine of these forces. The constant introduction of new types into service, however, soon proved to be a logistical nightmare as lack of standardisation and acquisition procedures led to a waste of resources considered unacceptable for a third world country like Peru and, therefore, the first steps were taken towards the unification of the two services, which finally arrived by the end of the 1920s.

The creation of the *Ministerio de Marina y Aviación* (Navy and Aviation Ministry, MMA) by Law No.6511, promulgated on 18 February 1929, during President Augusto B. Leguía's administration, was the first step undertaken by the Peruvian government to achieve the unification of the country´s existing military aviation services. This law provided the necessary legal framework for merging both the SAE and the CAN under a single command structure in a process that, due to the bureaucratic obstacles and the political chaos reigning in Perú during that period, ended nearly four years later on 3 July

With the help provided by MGP personnel, the remains of the ½-VG-6 are recovered from the muddy waters of the Nieva River. The Douglas was then shipped to Pucallpa, where it was stripped of all reusable parts and disposed of. Archive Humberto Currarino.

Eight Keystone K-55 "Pronto" were acquired during Augusto B. Leguía's administration in 1927. Strong and reliable, these aircraft provided the CAP´s Linea Aérea de la Montaña with an outstanding workhorse, flying tirelessly, equipped with floats or conventional landing gear, from its bases in San Ramón, Masisea, Pucallpa and Itaya to the numerous populations and army garrisons scattered along the vast Amazon forest. Archivo Histórico de la Marina via Gonzalo Maguiña.

The arrival of the O-38Ps to the combat area allowed the CAP to increase the pace of reconnaissance and bombing operations. Here an aircraft and its crew are being prepared for another sortie from their base in the Yacú River, February 1933. Archive Humberto Currarino.

A K-55 takes off from San Ramón in September of 1932. Archive IEHAP.

Washed by the waters of the Perené River in the high Amazon forest, Sotziki was a strategic connection centre for the CAP. A recently arrived Keystone "Pronto" serial I-R-5 is seen just before the beginning of its conversion to floats. Archive IEHAP.

1932, with the promulgation of a Supreme Decree creating the *Cuerpo de Aviación del Perú* (Peruvian Aviation Corps, CAP). The goal behind the creation of the CAP was to maximize the use of human resources and available materials of the existing aviation services under a single, unified command, with the inherent benefits of simplifying the logistics, reducing the maintenance workload, as well as improving the future acquisition processes under up-to-date parameters.

The CAP at the beginning of the Putumayo conflict

At the time of the Leticia incident, the *Cuerpo de Aviación del Perú* (Peruvian Aviation Corps, CAP) forces in the Putumayo area had the following structure and capabilities:

1. Command and personnel.

- Colonel Victor Ramos, Commander of *V División, Ejército del Perú* (V Division, Peruvian Army, EP) and commander of the Peruvian military forces in the Amazon theatre.
- Major Baltazar Montoya Monroe, CAP Commander-in-Chief.
- 20 officer pilots.

2. Air bases

- Teniente Guillermo Cornejo, Itaya River in Iquitos.
- San Ramón in Junín.
- Puca-Barranca (auxiliary base), Napo River in the Amazon forest.
- Pantoja (auxiliary base) Napo river in the western Amazon.
- Masisea auxiliary air base, in Ucayali.
- Pebas (auxiliary base), on the Amazon River.

3. Equipment.

The conflict found the Peruvians in possession of a diverse array of aircraft totalling 40 airframes in the form of:

- Eight Vought O2U-1E Corsair observation and light attack biplanes (7 operational)
- Ten Stearman C-3R liaison (5 operational)
- Two Boeing model 21 training seaplanes (1 operational)
- Two Change-Vought OU-1A observation biplanes (both operational)
- Four Douglas DT-2B for transport (1 operational)
- Seven Keystone K-55 Pronto for transport and liaison (3 operational)
- One Hamilton H-45 transport monoplane
- One Travelair E-4000 trainer
- Two Boeing model 40B-2 transport biplanes
- One Consolidated PT-3 Husky
- One Klemn Kl.25d liaison monoplane and
- One Udet U.12 Flamingo trainer (under repair)

With 25 aircraft in airworthy condition the CAP appeared on paper as a numerically superior force.

The most advanced and capable type in Perú at the time of the conflict was the Vought O2U-1E Corsair, twelve of which were purchased in July 1930. By 1932 a few had been lost in accidents and operational attrition, including one shot down by insurrectionist APRA elements during 1931, and the remainder split between Ancon and Las Palmas for advanced training. By September 1932, seven of

A nice aerial shot of Keystone serial I-R-4 flying over the Amazon forest landscape in the early thirties. Archivo Histórico de la Marina via Gonzalo Maguiña.

The crew of this Keystone, identified with serial I-R-1, seen visiting a populated center on the Pachitea river during the summer of 1932. Archivo Histórico de la Marina via Gonzalo Maguiña.

A beautiful shot of Hamilton H-45 serial I-R-10 assigned to the *Primera Escuadrilla de Reconocimiento* moored at Puca-Barranca forward base in late 1932. Archivo Histórico de la Marina via Gonzalo Maguiña.

At the time of the conflict I-R-10 was the only Hamilton H-45 on strength with the CAP, and it was reinforced with the arrival of a second machine in March of 1933. The H-45 had a stellar record service with the CAP and both airframes operated until past the year 1940. Archive IEHAP.

these machines were in airworthy condition, but not combat-ready due to lack of ammunition and technical problems with the feeding system for their Colt 7.65mm machine guns. Also, and perhaps even more important, there were only five sets of EDO type floats available for them.

The second most important aircraft in terms of importance were seven K-55 employed as liaison and transport aircraft between San Ramón and Iquitos. These aircraft were purchased in late 1926 by Commander Harold B.Grow, at the time head of the *Cuerpo de Aviadores Navales*, with the aim of establishing a transport unit in order to link the main cities of the country with the remote areas in the Peruvian Amazon forest. Four of these aircraft were based at Iquitos and provided the only viable communication and supply mechanism between this city and the hundreds of small populated areas scattered across the vastness of the Amazon.

The ten Stearman C-3R were purchased in July 1930 by the Peruvian government and employed in advanced training and liaison duties. Six were assigned to Las Palmas, operating under the command of the *Escuela Central de Aviación* and, from 1931, under the command of the *Escuadrilla de Transportes*. The remaining four were assigned to Ancón where, fitted with floats, they served as advanced trainers. The pair of Chance-Vought OU-1A were purchased in 1926 as part of the CAN re-equipment process and had been repaired and fitted with new engines in the early thirties. The other important aircraft in CAP inventory was a single Hamilton H-45 monoplane. Bought in 1930, this aircraft was assigned to Iquitos as a transport and was greatly appreciated by its crews due to its ruggedness and ease of maintenance. Regarding the remaining aircraft, these were trainers, liaison and transport types – some of them fitted with floats – purchased during the previous decade and in various states of preservation, but none of them suitable for first line service; they were scattered between Las Palmas, Ancon and San Ramón.

CAP problems were not restricted to the number of aircraft, but there was also a shortage of fuel, bombs and ammunition. While a

CAP officers portrayed in front of a Stearman C-3R in seaplane configuration at Teniente Carlos Huguet seaplane base in Ancon in late 1932. Archivo Histórico de la Marina via Gonzalo Maguiña.

Two Douglas DT-2B were converted to transports and assigned to the *Escuadrilla de Transportes* in 1931. However, due to their age and limited performance, these aircraft saw only limited service during the conflict with Colombia. Archivo Histórico de la Marina via Maguiña.

A Boeing model 21 seaplane seen low over the Pacific Ocean during a routine training flight. Inherited from the Naval Aviation Corps, the CAP still operated a handful of these aircraft at the beginning of the conflict, albeit they were all grounded by late 1933. Archive Humberto Currarino.

A Fairchild FW-2C from the CAP seen at Masisea airfield in April of 1933. Archive Humberto Currarino.

Several aircraft were leased to the Peruvian government by the Faucett Aviation Co. during the conflict, this Stinson SM-1D being one of them. It was later acquired by the CAP as a response to its transport requirements in the Amazon forest.

CAP Stinson SM-1 sporting the registration IV/6-TP-1B seen at Pucallpa airfield in Ucayali in 1934. Archivo Histórico de la Marina via Maguiña.

Bought in the year 1928 the Consolidated PT-3 "Husky" helped train several dozens of Peruvian airmen until its retirement from military service, soldiering on until late 1933. Archive IEHAP.

A number of Travelair S-6000B acquired by the CAP were fitted with floats to serve as transports in the Amazon region. Here Travelair serial V/6-TP-3B is returning to Itaya after a mission.

Alferez Carlos Huguet Base at Ancon.

Las Palmas on the early 30s.

Itaya air base in Iquitos.

Masisea base.

small factory for bombs and ammunition was set up at Las Palmas – CAP's main airbase – stocks remained low, particularly concerning explosive devices. As of 1 September, the stock of aviation bombs available at Las Palmas was:

- Fragmentation, 25 pounds: 50
- Fragmentation, 50 pounds: 103
- Hand grenades 50

It is worth noting that these devices had been effectively tested against hard surfaces like compact soil, steel and concrete, but not against water or soft terrain – an omission that would have direct consequences as will be explained in detail later on. Reserves of aviation fuel in Itaya and San Ramon – the main CAP bases in the east – were meagre, reaching a total of 2,637 and 925 imperial gallons (Imp Gal) respectively, insufficient to sustain the wide range of operations envisaged in the CAP operational planners' calculations.

The biggest disadvantage of the CAP against the Colombians, however, was the fact that not even one CAP combat crew had operational experience in the Amazon rain forest, due to the absence of a training program for that particular operational area, while in Colombia, the crews of SCADTA already had a wealth of knowledge of long endurance flights and operations over the jungle, which were vital for the development of the Colombian operations. Therefore, the only crews actually familiar with such an environment were a handful of liaison pilots from the *Linea Aérea de la Montaña* (or Mountain Airline, LAM), a transport unit operating between San Ramon and Iquitos. This, as we will see, proved to be a critical factor in the CAP's mounting losses sustained as the conflict developed.

Faced with the Government's decision to support the "patriots" occupying Leticia and Tarapacá, from 1 September onwards, the *Ministerio de Guerra* (or War Ministry – MG) and the *Ministerio de Marina y Aviación* (Navy and Aviation Ministry- MMA) senior staff issued the necessary arrangements to ensure the presence of military forces in the conflict area.

In the first place, orders were issued to repair the machine gun feeding systems on the entire Corsair fleet, with the aim of readying them for the aircrafts' departure for the operational theatre. This order coincided with the transfer by rail to Sotziki – located on the shore of the Perené River – of four sets of floats to be later fitted to the Voughts arriving from Lima, in order to allow these to take off from the river and proceed towards Iquitos following the course of the Ucayali River.

In the second place, the MMA ordered – as a matter of urgency – that the fuel, aviation oil and ammunition stocks on the diverse bases and auxiliary airfields located in the operations area needed to be increased. Finally, it was also ordered that the aircraft conducting transport and liaison flights between San Ramón, Masisea and Itaya were to receive – wherever possible – a defensive machine gun in the observer's position to provide defence against any likely attacks by enemy aircraft.

The National Collection

Aware of the need to meet the armed forces' rearmament requirements in order to face the upcoming operations against the Colombian offensive, and as the Congress seemed to be carrying endless debates to approve an increase of the country's foreign indebtedness, the Peruvian Government – as its Colombian counterpart – appealed for civilian support to obtain immediate funds aimed at the purchase of arms. Accordingly, a nationwide collection was organized under the responsibility of a so-called *Comité de la Colecta Nacional* (National Collection Committee- CCN).

Teniente Cornejo base at the Itaya River.

Air view of Masisea base on the Ucayali River.

Purchase of combat aircraft was the highest priority, followed by engines and spare parts for the aircraft already in service, so, after evaluation of the material immediately available, the *Comisión Técnica de la Defensa Nacional* (National Defence Technical Commission, CTDN)[14] requested the allocation of funds necessary for the purchase of:

- 15 Douglas O-38 reconnaissance / light bombers.
- 10 Curtiss model 35-A Hawk II fighters.
- 200 50 kg demolition bombs.
- 600 25 kg demolition bombs.
- 1200 25 kg fragmentation bombs.

Regarding the aircraft, the decision was heavily influenced by their immediate availability and the fact that both models shared the same engine[15], an unavoidable requirement according to the procedures for aircraft acquisition established in 1929. The CCN, however, denied the request arguing that the total cost of these purchases exceeded the amount of money gathered by the collection so far, and that the CCN did not have Government authorization to go deeper into debt. Additionally, the CCN pointed out that their funds could only be used for the purchase of aircraft, not spares or engines. Nevertheless, CCN granted the funds for the purchase of three Curtiss Hawk II and six Douglas O-38. The contracts for the purchase of these aircraft were signed on 12 and 17 October 1932, respectively, and amounted for the sum of $252,870 USD, which included a complete set of floats for each aircraft. Additionally, the Commission authorized a further $45,000 USD for the purchase of five Pratt & Whitney R-1340C-1 Wasp engines, as well as five sets of floats for the Vought Corsair biplanes.

These purchases of aircraft, although modern and effective, would prove insufficient – especially for fighters – to fulfil the CAP's operational requirements for the upcoming campaign, particularly in view of the larger number of aircraft purchased by Colombia.

Chapter 6
GROUND AND NAVAL ORDERS OF BATTLE

Colombian Army

The Colombian Army was reorganized several times since the beginning of the 20th Century, despite this it had always had a strength of about 400 officers and 6,000 soldiers, a small force for such a big country. The Decree 340 of 1925 ordered the last reorganization before the conflict; the changes stated on it were applied slowly and finished only by 1930. The plan was to have five divisions organized as follows:

1st Division with headquarters at Bogotá, with three infantry battalions, a cavalry group, an artillery group and a train battalion.

2nd Division at Barranquilla with three infantry battalions and a train battalion.

3rd Division at Cali with three infantry battalions, a cavalry group, an artillery group and a train battalion.

4th Division at Medellín, with three infantry battalions and a sapper battalion.

5th Division at Bucaramanga with three infantry battalions and a cavalry squadron.

Also, subordinate directly to the War Ministry was the Honour Guard Battalion of the Republic's President, a guard platoon for the ammunition factory, a special infantry unit for the Amazon border, an aviation ground platoon, the military aviation and the riverine war flotilla.

According to this organization, each infantry unit had 21 officers, 64 NCOs and 304 soldiers, each cavalry unit 21 officers, 68 NCOs and 224 soldiers, an artillery unit 21 officers, 64 NCOs and 232 soldiers, the sapper unit 16 officers, 48 NCOs and 189 soldiers and the train units 12 officers, 38 NCOs and 156 soldiers.

After the delimitation of the border with Peru in 1930, the *Jefatura de Fronteras* (Border Command) and the *Unidad de Colonización* (Colonization Unit) was created with four officers and 43 soldiers, dependant from the War Ministry, and sent to the Putumayo, being at Caucayá when Leticia was occupied.

In 1931 a new reorganization took place under Decree 1842, with the divisions replaced by brigades, as their real strength was smaller than a division. Thus, the order of battle of the Colombian Army when the conflict erupted was as follows[16]:

Colombian soldier in 1932, with the equipment used during the conflict.

Colombian soldiers deployed to the Putumayo region.

1º Brigada, headquarters at Bogotá.
Batallón de Infantería Bolívar 1, at Tunja.
Batallón de Infantería Sucre 2, at Bogotá.
Batallón de Infantería Bárbula 13, at Neiva.
Grupo de Caballería Páez 1, at Bogotá.
Grupo de Artillería Bogotá 1, at Bogotá.
Batallón de Ferrocarrileros Mejía 1, at Flandes.
2º Brigada at Barranquilla.
Batallón de Infantería Nariño 5, at Barranquilla.
Batallón de Infantería Córdova 6, at Santa Marta.
Batallón de Infantería Cartagena 7, at Cartagena.
Batallón de Ferrocarrileros Albán 2, at Ciénaga.
3º Brigada at Cali.
Batallón de Infantería Pichincha 10, at Cali.
Batallón de Infantería Junín 11, at Popayán.
Batallón de Infantería Boyacá 12, at Pasto.
Grupo de Caballería Cabal 3, at Ipiales.
Batería Palacé 3, at Buga.
Compañía de Ferrocarrileros Soublette 3, at Armenia.
4º Brigada at Medellín.
Batallón de Infantería Girardot 8, at Medellín.
Batallón de Infantería Ayacucho 9, at Manizales.
Batallón de Infantería Bomboná 14, at Líbano.
Batallón de Zapadores Caldas 1, at Ibagué.
5º Brigada at Bucaramanga.
Batallón de Infantería Ricaurte 3, at Bucaramanga.
Batallón de Infantería Santander 4, at Cúcuta.
Batallón de Infantería García Rovira 15, at Pamplona.
Escuadrón de Caballería Maza 5, at Concepción.

Colombian gun boats at Caucayá.

The destroyer *Caldas* of the Colombian Navy.

The Colombian gun boat *Cartagena* at the time of the conflict.

View of the gun boat Cartagena after the conflict, when she received some modifications in the upper structure and weapons.

The Colombian gun boat *Córdova* purchased in France.

The Colombian Navy transport vessel *Nariño*.

The gun boat *Pichincha* of the Colombian Navy.

The transport *Boyacá* of the Colombian Navy.

Troops subordinate to the War Ministry

The Border Command in the Amazon, a Colonization Company in the Amazon, a platoon of guards at the ammunition factory, the aviation ground platoon, the military aviation and the riverine flotilla.

Together with the modernization of the training and structure of the Army, from 1928 a modernization program began for the weapons, a total of 5,000 Mauser model 1924 rifles, ten Schwarzlose 7mm machine guns, 2 Madsen machine guns for the infantry and two for the aviation, spares for the Mauser model 1912 in use since 1914 and 1,000 shells for the four Ehrhardt guns – acquired in 1914 – had been received by 1932. Also, the force had, as artillery, 4 Bange and 2 Krupp guns and six Maxim machine guns.

One of the main problems was the lack of officers, as only between 12 and 30 graduated from the *Escuela Militar de Cadetes* (Cadet Military School) and none of the units were at full strength. In total, there were about 400 officers and 6,000 soldiers. Also, the units were mainly distributed against internal threats rather than foreign ones, as they were in the centre of the country and far from the borders.

The forces on the southern border were under the III Brigade, based in Cali, having three infantry battalions at Cali, Popayán and Pasto, plus an artillery and an engineer battalion. There were also small detachments in the departments of Putumayo, Caquetá and Amazonas, at Puerto Asís, Puerto Ospina, Caucaya, El Encanto, La Tagua and La Pedrera, with a total of 150 men, plus 21 policemen evacuated from Leticia.

The *Destacamento Putumayo* (Putumayo Detachment) was created on 15 September 1932 under command of Colonel Roberto Rico, based at Caucayá, having 154 officers and NCOs and 400 men. Under their command were the ships of that detachment and later the three Junkers F13 from SCADTA. From October 1932, by Decree 1745, the detachment consisted of a Staff, a transmissions platoon, a medical platoon, two infantry and one engineer battalions, an artillery battery

The hospital ship *Yamary* used by the Colombians.

and two transport units, and by 14 February 1933 reached about 35 officers and 600 NCOs and soldiers at Caucayá and 15 officers and 350 men in the other posts, such as El Encanto, Puerto Ospina, Chavaco, La Tagua, Potosí, Peña Blanca, Mondar, Delicias, Puerto Asís, Puerto Boy and La Pedrera.

Naval forces

Colombia had a very tiny Navy at the beginning of the 20th Century, subordinate to the War Ministry, despite their large coastline on the Caribbean and the Pacific Ocean, mainly because for many years the governments were focused on the internal problems, rather than on any external threat. By 1907 the Naval School was created at the steamer *Marroquín*, having as a naval force the light cruisers *Pinzón* and *Cartagena* and the gunboats *Hércules* and *Boyacá*, but by 1910 the school was closed and the ships were sold. The force was reorganized in 1925 as part of the Army, with the construction in France of three small patrol vessels of 120 tons, the *Pichincha*, *Carabobo* and *Junín*, each armed with a 75mm gun on the bow and a 37mm gun on the stern.

To increase the force, on 31 August 1929 a contract was signed with Yarrow shipyard in the UK for the construction of three gunboats of 142 tons, baptized *Cartagena*, *Barranquilla* and *Santa Marta*. They were each armed with two Bofors 75mm guns, an Oerlikon of 20mm and four Vickers 7mm machine guns. After sailing from the UK, they arrived at Puerto Colombia, near Barranquilla, in 1930 and formed the *Flotilla Fluvial de Guerra* at the Magdalena River, together with the gunboat *Colombia*, which was a stern-wheel transport steamer modified with weapons and later re-baptized *Presidente Mosquera*.

For use in the Amazon basin, in 1928 the government purchased from Manaus in Brazil, a 140-ton transport and, despite belonging to the Industry Ministry, was used by the Army. In 1933, it was transferred to the War Ministry. There was also the launch *Huila*, purchased also at Manaus, around 1919, and with a displacement of 80 tons, integrated to the *Flotilla del Amazonas* in 1932.

In August 1931, it was decided to transfer the gunboats *Cartagena* and *Santa Marta* to Caucayá in the Putumayo, to increase the presence on the Amazon. The trip was a very long one, as the riverine vessels must go out to sea and sail from Barranquilla, in the mouth of the Magdalena river, to Belém do Pará in the mouth of the Amazon in Brazil, and from there to Manaus and finally to Caucayá. There they formed the *Flotilla del Amazonas*, created on 31 August 1931 together with the *Flotilla del Magdalena*, with the remining ships.

With the eruption of the conflict, the Colombian government decided to buy new ships to deploy on the Amazon, as all troop movements and support needed to be made by river. In addition, ocean going vessels were needed to defend the coasts against any possible action by the Peruvian Navy, which was far more powerful.

Initially, they tried to buy two 9,000-ton cruisers in Spain, but this was abandoned as they don't have the personnel to man them. An attempt to buy the Spanish cruiser *Eduardo Dato* also failed, as Spain declared neutrality in the conflict and couldn't sell them weapons.

Finally, two ships were purchased in France, one of 1,700 tons, baptized *Mosquera* (the former one had sunk at Cartagena) and armed with two Krupp 88mm and two 20mm guns and ten 7mm machine guns. The other was of 600 tons and was named *Córdova*.

Also, the support to the Putumayo area by road reached only to the city of Florencia or to Puerto Asís, as there were no roads beyond that point into the Amazon. Each of these points were more than 200 kilometres from Caucayá. From Florencia, equipment and troops had to be taken by boat from the nearby town of Venecia and from there to Tagua, a small town on the left bank of the Caquetá River, 20 kilometres from Caucayá. From Puerto Asís it needed to be taken through the Putumayo directly to Caucayá.

For this task, the launch *SinchiRoca* was captured from the Peruvians. The *Wayna Capac* was another launch captured from the Peruvians at Caucayá, was of 39 tons, and towed the barge *Bolivar*, of 40 tons. The *SinchiRoca* had a displacement of 48 tons. The two launches belonged to the Anglo South American Bank, who used them at Iquitos, and were officially rented to it on 12 January 1933 and operated until 3 July of that year. The launch *Emita*, of 20 tons and Brazilian ownership, was also briefly rented to carry loads from Puerto Asís to Caucayá until early April. When the owner was returning the *Emita* to Brazil, it was attacked by Peruvian planes, causing one dead and three wounded, with the launch having to return to Caucayá.

Meanwhile, in early 1933, a ship of 68.9 meters long, baptized *Bogotá*, was bought in France. This ship was armed with an 88mm Krupp gun, two 75mm Bofors guns and two 13.2mm machine guns. Meanwhile, at Manaus, another ship, the *Yamary*, a 300-ton barge,

The Peruvuan Navy supply ship BAP *Huallaga* on the Yubinete River.

was bought and transformed into a hospital ship which was to be towed by the *Bogotá*. Also, a yacht called *Flying Fox* was bought in the USA and sailed to the Amazonas, renamed *Mariscal Sucre*, armed with two 75mm guns and five machine guns, arriving in Belém on 5 March 1933.

After the reception of the aircraft from the US and Germany, the force in the Amazon was also later enlarged with the gunboats *Pichincha* and *Barranquilla,* and the transport *Boyacá*, purchased in the United States and used to carry 741 men (539 infantry and 202 from the artillery) under command of General Efraín Rojas, from the Caribbean coast to the war zone, through the Amazon River, together with the new *Mosquera* and *Córdova*, arriving in Belém do Pará, on the Amazon River mouth on 24 December and sailing through the Amazonas from 28 December 1932. The *Barranquilla* had to enter Curaçao to repair damage and joined the rest of the force at the mouth of the Putumayo on 8 February. This force was referred to as *"Expedición Punitiva"* (Punitive Expedition), under the command of General Alfredo Vásquez Cobo and was the main force of the *Destacamento Amazonas*. At Manaus they were joined by the transport *Nariño*, converted into hospital ship there, and they left that city on 17 January. They reached the town of Tefé by 25 January, on the mouth of the Caquetá River, but decided to wait for the *Barranquilla*. On the 26th they saw the two Peruvian gunboats *América* and *Napo*, which were averted by a gunshot from the *Mosquera*, but the Colombians couldn't determine if they took the Putumayo or the Amazon. The small fleet then moved to the town of Tonantins, close to the mouth of the Putumayo. By 12 February 1933 this force reached a place called Cardozo, near Ipiranga, on Brazilian territory, close to the border with Colombia on the Putumayo River.

In addition to the previously mentioned purchases, the Colombian government acquired, from Portugal, two destroyers, from a total of five being built at the time by the Vickers Armstrong and Yarrow Company in Lisbon for the Portuguese Navy. These ships, identified with the names *Duero* and *Tajo*, were renamed as the *Antioquia* and *Caldas*, and were armed with four 120mm Vickers guns, three 40mm Bofors guns, two Weymouth torpedo launchers, and depth charges. These vessels, the most powerful ships of the Colombian navy, after their arrival in Cartagena on 14 May 1934, were assigned to the patrol of Colombian territorial waters in the Pacific Ocean.

Other ships acquired during the war were the 12,000-ton transport ship *Commercial Traveller*, renamed *Cúcuta*, which was purchased in the United States and arrived in Puerto Colombia on 2 May 1934, departing to Belém the next day carrying the Camilo Torres battalion, together with the *Ciudad de Pasto,* a ship rented to the United Fruit Company, and the tanker *Cabimas*. As the conflict was finished while the ships were sailing on the Amazon, they left the battalion at Manaus and the *Cúcuta* went to the USA to be converted onto a training ship. Finally, it is worth mentioning that the launch *Wayna Capac* was returned to Peru in late 1934 as part of the peace agreement.

Perú

Ground Forces

By the beginning of the 20th Century, the Peruvian Army was helped in its organization and training by a French military mission, which withdrew with the beginning of the First World War but returned in 1919 and lasted until 1939. The main rifle of the force was the 7.65mm Mauser, while the artillery had 75mm Krupp Model 1894 mountain guns and Model 1905 field guns, joined after 1919 by Schneider Model 1906 field and 1909 mountain guns, also of 75mm, and 105mm Schneider Model 1928 howitzers. Also, Hotchkiss Model 1914 machine guns were added, followed by examples from Madsen and, by the time of the Putumayo conflict, some Czech ZB-30 models. Stokes-Brandt mortars of 60mm and 81mm, as well as 20mm Oerlikon anti-aircraft guns were also received during the conflict.

From 1926 the force was re-organized by German General Wilhelm Faupel, having by that time 1,020 officers and 6,536 other ranks organized into 20 infantry battalions, one company of mounted infantry, five cavalry regiments, five artillery regiments and two engineer companies, in five divisions[17]. Faupel organized the force into light divisions, each with four infantry battalions and an artillery group, to which a cavalry regiment and/or an engineer battalion might be attached if necessary. Eight divisions were then created with one in

The Peruvian Navy Amazon Flotilla.

each of the five military regions, with the first, third and fifth also each having one of the new divisions.

Thus, as this modification was not yet totally implemented, the Peruvian Army had, by 1932, an organization that included eight infantry regiments, plus two battalions. Also, four artillery regiments, an artillery group, four cavalry regiments, an escort regiment, a company of heavy machine guns, two engineer companies, two horse barracks and a transmission section. The force had 1,065 officers and 7,980 soldiers[18].

By 1 September 1932, the Peruvian forces on the border with Colombia were commanded by Colonel Víctor Ramos, head of the V Division, with headquarters at Iquitos. Under his command he had the *Regimiento de Infantería Mixto No.17*, two infantry battalions, an artillery battery, a sapper section and the services of intendency, armament, sanitation, recruiting, military justice and transmissions. They had small garrisons at Curaray, Pantoja, Nashiño, Güepí, Puerto Arturo, Barranca, Puerto Alayza, Chimbote, Corrientes and Puerto Inca, with a strength of about 1,700 men. They also used the Huapanas, Iquitos and Portillo transport vessels to move in the area, as roads were very few.

The main garrisons were at Iquitos, with 900 men, at Puerto Arturo, with 15 officers and 480 men, Cabo Pantoja, with eight officers and 217 men, and Güepí, with three officers and 60 men. Close to the border with Ecuador there were another 75 soldiers, and in the garrison at Pantoja there were another 45 men. After the first actions, most of these garrisons were reinforced with extra men and supplies, including the material carried by the transport *Marañón*, which sailed from the Pacific coast to the Amazon and then to Iquitos.

Naval Forces

After losing the war with Chile in 1883, the Peruvian Navy almost disappeared. Rebuilding began two years later, but the big growth of the force began by 1904.

At the beginning of the conflict, the *Marina de Guerra del Perú* (Peruvian Navy) had a fleet of two 3400-ton British-built cruisers, BAP *Almirante Grau* and *Coronel Bolognesi*, both ordered in 1905 and armed with two 152mm guns and eight 76mm ones, as well as the gunship BAP *Lima* – which was built during the war with Chile – with four 102mm guns and eight 3 pounder ones, the training ship BAP *Constitución* and the destroyer BAP *Teniente Rodríguez*, acquired in France in 1910 (the former *Actée* of the French Navy) as well as four submarines built by Electric Boat Co. in the United States, called R-1, R-2, R-3 and R-4 respectively. The submarines were commissioned between 1926 and 1928, and replaced the French built *Ferré* and *Palacios*, which, entering service in 1911, were the first Latin American submarines. All these units were based in the port of Callao.

In addition, for the defence of the Amazon, the Navy had the so-called Amazon River Fleet, based on the Itaya river in Iquitos and was composed of the following units:

- Two gunboats: BAP *America*, a 240-ton river vessel with a maximum speed of 11 knots, built in 1904 and armed with four 37mm Vickers Armstrong guns; and the BAP *Napo*, built in 1925 and armed with three Vickers Armstrong QF guns of 37mm.
- Ten launches: the *Iquitos*, built in 1875 and armed with a 37mm Vickers Armstrong QF gun; the *Cahuapanas*, launched in 1880. Other boats assigned to the Amazon Flotilla included the *Callao*, *Águila*, *Bora*, *Luella*, *Leticia*, *Auxiliadora* and the *Atahualpa*.
- Four small steamers: the *Estefita*, *San Miguel*, *Huallaga* and *Meteoro*. During the conflict, a river steamer called *San Pablo*, launched in 1880, was also pressed into service with the Navy and named *Colonel Portillo*.

These units were operated by approximately 300 men of all ranks, with 800 rifles and half a dozen Vickers 37mm and 47mm guns at their disposal. In total, the Peruvian Navy had 189 officers, 451 NCOs, 1,025 sailors and 110 cadets at the Naval School.

After Colombia purchased their two destroyers during the conflict, the Peruvian Navy bought two Russian-built vessels from Estonia, baptized *Almirante Guise* and *Almirante Villar*, which were sent to the mouth of the Amazon to join the *Almirante Grau* and two submarines that were sent there in a failed attempt to blockade the entrance of the river to the Colombians. Two gunboats were also ordered in the United States after the conflict began, named *Amazonas* and *Loreto*, while the transports *Rimac* and the oiler *Pariñas* were purchased, but all arrived after the end of the conflict.

Chapter 7
DEPLOYMENT AND FIRST ACTIONS

Colombian first movements

On 3 September, just two days after the incidents in Leticia and Tarapacá, the German pilot Hans von Engel carried out a risky flight from La Florencia to the Colombian garrison of Caucayá, in the Putumayo. On board the Junkers F13 serialled 203 and named *Boyacá*, was Colombian Army Colonel Luiz Azevedo, whose mission was to inform the commanders of the border garrisons of the situation between Colombia and Peru. Accommodated in this small garrison was the Peruvian boat *Wayna Capac*, a river transport vessel of the Peruvian Navy, which was captured, along with its crew, by the garrison's troops moments after the *Boyacá* took off from the river towards its next destination.

After becoming aware of the beginning of the crisis and the issuance of legal provisions to activate and reinforce military aviation, Colombian aviation began to make flights to the south of the country, transferring equipment, fuel, medicines and weapons to bases close to the border with the purpose of increasing their readiness.

The Army Aviation decided to recover the use of the airfield of Flandes, which was next to the hydroplane base of SCADTA, to prepare the crews that would be sent to the Amazon. There, also the three Junkers F13 delivered by SCADTA were modified with openings on the top of the rear cabin to install old Darne machine guns, and openings in the floor to drop bombs and artillery shells modified with fins to make them fall vertically.

The operations started on 4 September with the transfer of two Wild Xs, identified with the serials 105 and 108, from the base of Madrid to Flandes. The next day Captain Camilo Daza took off from Flandes on his way to Neiva aboard Wild serial 105, carrying fuel, while Captain Lema Posada flew aboard Wild serial 108 on the same route.

The operations continued on day 6 with the transfer, between Madrid and Neiva, of the Wild aircraft serialled 106, piloted by Major Benjamín Méndez, who flew with Lieutenant Diego Muñoz. Meanwhile, the Wild X number 105 remained in Neiva at the same time as the 108, piloted by Captain Lema Posada, flew from Neiva to Florencia and back. The following day, this operation was repeated by Captain Motto aboard the Wild 108 while, again, Captain Daza remained in Neiva with the Wild serialled 105.

Eight Swiss built Wild-Comte X reconnaissance and light attack biplanes were bought by Colombia from the Swiss military mission during the late twenties. According to some sources only three of these aircraft remained in service with Colombian military aviation by 1 September 1932. Archive Dan Hagedorn.

A rare view of the Curtiss D-12 Falcon christened as Ricaurte after the Colombian military aviation hero Antonio Ricaurte. Originally in private ownership, the Ricaurte was donated to the AM at the beginning of the conflict. Archive Dan Hagedorn.

On the 8th, Captain Motto flew between Neiva and Flandes aboard the Wild serial 108, while Captain Daza remained in Neiva with the

Among the few aircraft in AMC strength were three of the reliable Curtiss model 51 Fledgling trainers employed for elementary instruction. Archive Dan Hagedorn.

Comte Wild X of the Colombian Air Arm.

The W33 "Cundinamarca" at Barranquilla with the F13 C-24 "Antioquia" and the Dornier Wal C-28 "Colombia", among other planes. Archive Javier Franco.

One of the F13, the 202, delivered to the Colombian Air Arm for operations on a river to the south of Colombia during the conflict with Peru. The F13 were of great value, as they performed reconnaissance, transport, medical evacuation and bombing missions. Archive Mauricio Umaña.

Junkers F13 FAC 203 at a river on the Amazon region, together with the Fokker Super Universal C-44 "Medellín" delivered by SCADTA, which received serial 205 and, behind, one of the K43. The Super Universal was lost on 15 December 1932 during a flight between Girardot and Bogotá

View of Caucayá from the Colombian Junkers K43 serialled 403.

One of the Junkers K43 of the Colombian Air Arm at Flandes.

aircraft number 105. Aircraft 106 moved from Madrid to Flandes, under the command of Captain Andres Diaz, carrying a Madsen machine gun, a Scarff turret, four ammunition bags, as well as toilet implements for SCADTA. This pilot was ordered to remain at that location until further notice. Operations continued on the 9th with a flight between Flandes and Madrid by Captain Diaz aboard the Wild 108 while Captain Daza did the same on board 105 from Neiva on his way to Flandes with the mission of picking up a starter. Meanwhile Major Mendez Rey boarded a train bound for Flandes to return, in the afternoon, aboard the Wild serial 106. During the afternoon, Lieutenant Garcia headed by land from Madrid to Flandes carrying a machine gun, as well 18 pumps to equip the aircraft of SCADTA. Upon completion of this task the Lieutenant was incorporated as an observer of the Junkers F13 serial 201.

On 10 September 1932, a portable hangar was moved from Madrid by 1st Sergeant Rubio and installed in Neiva. Four days later, Captain Motto flew from Flandes to Madrid aboard the Wild serial

A nice in-flight shot of a Boeing model 40B-2 serial 2-R-2 from the *Segunda Escuadrilla de Reconocimiento* flying over the typical landscape found in the operations theatre. Archive Amaru Tincopa.

A Boeing model 40B-2 being refuelled at San Ramon in the summer of 1933. The T prefix identified the aircraft as a transport from June 1933 after the introduction of a number of organizational rearrangements that were part of the Peruvian Air Corps reorganization process launched in that month. Archive IEHAP.

Taken from one of the nurse boats that provided support to CAP units deployed in the Amazon, this image shows the return of Vought serial 2-E-4 after completing another sortie. Archive Humberto Currarino.

Vought 5-E-6 leaves its hangar at Itaya before leaving bound for the operations area in December of 1932. Note the correctly applied Peruvian national colours on the rudder section. Archive IEHAP.

Sub Officer Mario Dolci was the gunner aboard 5-E-6 flown by 2nd Lt. Secada during the aerial engagement of February 14 known as the "Tarapacá combat". Archive Humberto Currarino.

103 carrying Lt. Garcia as passenger. Another mission took off from Madrid on the way to Techo (Bogotá), in the Wilds serials 103 and 108 piloted by Captain Diaz and Lieutenant Santa Maria, respectively. The first carrying machine guns and ammunition, while the second carried two officers of the Military School. After completing these tasks both aircraft proceeded to Flandes, where Captain Diaz delivered the aircraft 103 to Captain Motto so that he could return to Madrid. Meanwhile, Lieutenant Santa Maria returned to Flandes after leaving his passengers in Techo.

On 15 September, the aircraft 105 commanded by Captain Daza,

Yubinete River mouth, January 1933. A CAP Vought Corsair identified with serial 5-E-2 returns to base after a fruitless armed reconnaissance mission over the Putumayo. A second machine is visible in the background. Archive Humberto Currarino.

A Vought Corsair begins its take off run from the Yubinete River, a Putumayo tributary, whose mouth is located approximately 100km from Leticia. Archive Humberto Currarino.

CAP personnel handle the wings of Vought serial 5-E-6 in order to place it inside its natural "hangar". Yubinete river mouth, January 1933. Archive Humberto Currarino.

For defensive purposes the CAP Vought Corsairs were equipped with a drum fed Browning 7.65mm machine gun mounted on a Scarff ring. Archive Humberto Currarino.

moved from Neiva to Potosí taking a doctor as a passenger, and Captain Diaz as an observer. The aircraft returned to its home base after leaving the doctor in Caucayá, on the first flight of a Wild X equipped with floats to the area of operations. On 16 September, Lt. Santa Maria, aboard the Wild 108, took off from Madrid and followed the Neiva-Potosi-Neiva itinerary.

Meanwhile, the Junkers F13 *Cúcuta* took off from Flandes with the German pilot Klotz, Captain Diaz and the mechanic Simon Butz, to practise throwing bombs on the field of Camalá, contiguous to that base, on the first bombing tests performed with the F13s.

At the same time, the Wild X serialled 106, piloted by Mayor Mendez and with the mechanic Mr. Diaz as passenger, took off from Madrid heading for Neiva and then to Potosí, where the mechanic remained, and the aircraft and its pilot later returned to Madrid. Also, Captain Daza, who was picked up by Lieutenant Santa Maria in Wild number 105, was transferred back from Potosí to Neiva. Once back in that town, Daza and Santa Maria made numerous flights between Neiva and Potosí transporting the bombs that they had in their

Vought serial 5-E-6 awaits a new mission hidden under the natural concealment provided by the Amazon forest. The two white rectangular patches that can be seen right after the serial number are repairs to damage to the fabric caused by bullet holes, a vivid example of the hard fighting sustained over the green inferno. Archive Amaru Tincopa.

Vought serial 5-E-6 seen at Sotziki shortly after its arrival from San Ramon and prior to the conversion to floats, a step required to complete its deployment to the front line in the Amazon. Archive Humberto Currarino.

CAP crews pose next to Douglas ½-VG-2 during a pause in operations. Puca-Barranca, April 1933. Archive Amaru Tincopa.

custody.

This airlift launched by the Colombian Military Aviation to the Southern Operations Theatre, continued on 17 September when the high command ordered Mayor Mendez to transfer, on board the Wild X serial 106, radio sets from Neiva to Altamira and Potosí. Meanwhile Captain Motto, together with Lt. Garcia, moved parts from Madrid to Neiva, then headed to Flandes. Later that day, Captain Garcia flew from Flandes to Madrid aboard the Wild X 103, while Lt. Santa Maria did the same from Neiva to Potosí carrying radio equipment aboard the Wild X serial 108. These operations were repeated until the end of the month. The flight of 23 September in which two aircraft, a Wild X identified with serial 104, piloted by Captain Gómez, and a Curtiss Fledgling with serial 17, flew over the city of Bogotá for publicity purposes for the National Defence Loan that had been launched at that time, is worthy of mention. These activities of flight in support of the Defence Loan were repeated the following day over the towns of the so-called Sabana, with the participation of the Wild X 103.

Meanwhile, on 22 September, Captain Díaz and mechanic Hunter tested dropping bombs with the Wild X serialled 105 at Madrid, on the first use of the model for that purpose.

Douglas ½-VG-4 and its crew returns from an armed reconnaissance sortie. Early criticism from CAP crews about the aircraft being unpowered had its origin in the fact that 87 octane fuel for its engine – which was the octane rating recommended by the factory- was not available in Perú at the time, leaving the aircraft to be flown with the lower 84 octane fuel instead, with the inherent reduction in the engine output. Archive IEHAP.

Douglas serial ½-VG-4 returns to its base in Pebas after another armed reconnaissance sortie. This particular aircraft was lost on May 10 1933 after being damaged in combat with Colombian Hawks. Archivo Histórico de la Marina via Gonzalo Maguiña.

CAP personnel stand on top of one of this O-38P's large EDO floats during a pause of operations from the Yacu river mouth. The intense use of these airframes is evidenced by the wear on the fuselage. Archive Humberto Currarino.

Crew members from Douglas ½-VG-2 are taken to their aircraft by the means of a small boat. Pebas, March of 1933. Archive IEHAP.

A nice shot of ½-VG-3 moored at the Yacu river forward base in April of 1933. Wong Archives via Gonzalo Magiña.

The crew of Douglas serial ½-VG-3 prepares to take off from Pebas forward base in order to fly an armed reconnaissance sortie over the Putumayo in early May 1933. The aircraft is armed with four 25lbs bombs. Archive IEHAP.

Liaison and supply operations between Madrid, Flandes and the bases on the periphery of the Amazon continued throughout the following months, establishing a line between Madrid and Potosí, served twice a week with the Wild X, besides other flights according to need.

The Junkers F13s, W33 and the Hamilton H-45, were deployed to the south from Flandes as they had longer range and their crews were experienced in using floats, with the first stop at Potosí and then on to Caucayá. This would then be the main deployment base, to where troops were sent from the city of Neiva by ground transport, thence via the Orteguaza and Caquetá Rivers, and then from La Tagua over land to Caucayá. From this small town, the Junkers began to support the nearby outposts of El Encanto, Puerto Ospina and Puerto Asís, the first on the central route to Tarapacá and Leticia, the others to the west of Caucayá. The Junkers also performed armed reconnaissance

A Douglas O-38P and a Curtiss model 35A Hawk II seen at Puca-Barranca base in the Napo river during a lull in operations in April of 1933. Archive IEHAP.

A pair of "Prontos" seen at Cabo Pantoja garrison in late 1932. Archivo Histórico de la Marina via Gonzalo Magiña.

A busy day at Teniente Cornejo seaplane base in the Itaya river. Several aircraft assigned to the *Linea Aérea de la Montaña* can be seen in this image. Archivo Histórico de la Marina via Gonzalo Maguiña.

missions to look for possible Peruvian troops on Colombian territory along that part of the border, while an advance to the conflict area was being prepared. They were the basis of the *Escuadrilla Aérea del Sur* of the Colombian Air Arm.

A reconnaissance flight was made by von Engel to La Pedrera, near the border with Brazil and to the north of the conflict area, as some rumours stated that there were problems in that zone too, but the flight showed nothing unusual there, and preparations for the construction of an airfield there were started. Meanwhile, Herbert Boy performed a flight with the F13 serialled 202 to the outpost of El Encanto, on the Caraparaná River, a tributary of the Putumayo and near the Peruvian post of Puerto Arturo, 300 kilometers to the southeast of Caucayá, to carry supplies and discover the situation there.

On another mission performed by Boy in that area, 100km upriver of Puerto Arturo, he found the Peruvian Navy gunships *Napo* and *América*, whose crew opened fire against the plane with light guns, scoring one hit on the F13. Despite the ships being an easy target for the F13, as they were stranded in the river and couldn't move, he did not have orders to attack. As the only supplies to El Encanto were carried by the F13s, the Peruvians deployed a team with a machine gun near the position to try to shoot the plane down, but they had to retreat before another flight was made, as they were short on supplies.

While the Junkers were operating in the south, training for eleven new pilots began at Madrid on 19 October with Fledglings 15 and 16 – keeping 17 as reserve – as the plane had received an extra fuel tank.

On 1st December 1932, by Decree 2065 the military aviation was organized into the *Dirección General de Aviación Militar*, as the force was growing fast and needed a proper organization. Meanwhile, the government requisitioned SCADTA's base at Buenaventura on 26 January 1933, by Decree 131, as it was needed for the protection of the harbours on the Pacific coast against any attempted attack by the Peruvians, creating the *Base Aérea Buenaventura* and the *Escuela de Hidroaviación*, which would include the *Escuadrilla Aeronaval del Pacífico*, the first attempt to create the Naval Aviation. Also, SCADTA's facilities in Cartagena were requisitioned by Decree 1475 at the end of 1932, and was activated in early 1933, when the Peruvian cruiser *Almirante Grau* and other vessels sailed north from Lima and crossed the Panama Canal in April. It was thought they were going to attack Cartagena, but in fact they went to the Amazon River to support their fleet on the operations area near Leticia.

The new planes began to arrive by the end of 1932, with the K43s receiving civil serials C-57 to 59 for their first flights, changed to the military serials 401 to 403 when they were deployed south. They were equipped with two dorsal positions for machine guns and could carry bombs under the fuselage and wings. The new Wals became 603 and 604 and arrived at Barranquilla on 1 December 1932 aboard the steamer *Heinz Horn* and were destined to Buenaventura, together with some of the W34 and K43, the Dornier C 2A and the Consolidated P2Y-1C. Facilities for their operation were also prepared at Palestina, Guapí, Tumaco, Utria and Sautatá, most of them already being used by SCADTA. The first Wal, together with one F13, one K43 and three Curtiss Hawk were deployed to La Pedrera, with the support of the *Nariño* hospital vessel. On 24 December 1932 a K43, commanded by German pilot Hans Werner, took the Colombian Minister of War to Neiva.

The Peruvian CAP in the area of operations

Accompanying the build-up of forces for the upcoming campaign and following requests from the V Division's high command in charge of all ground, naval and air forces present in the Putumayo, the CAP began to launch reconnaissance and liaison sorties over the operational area, employing the few LAM (*Línea Aérea de Montaña*) aircraft available. Accordingly, on 3 September, Keystone K-55 serial CAP I-R-6 took off from Itaya bound for Leticia, flown by Sub Lieutenant Rafael Dañino, carrying Petty Officer Alejandro Casquiel as mechanic/gunner and the chief of the Health Service from V Division as passenger. Lt. Dañino's orders were to overfly Leticia to confirm the presence of Peruvian forces and then fly his passenger to the Puerto Arturo garrison, located north of Leticia on the western bank of the Putumayo River,

Colombian military aviation received in 1928 eight Wilde-Comte X, serialled 101 to 108 and were used for liaison during the conflict.

Thirty Curtiss Model 35A Hawk II were purchased by Colombia as fighters, to be used both on wheels and floats.

The Colombian Hawks were used on floats during the conflict, which reduced their performance considerably.

Three Curtis BT-32 Condor were purchased by Colombia after the conflict, all equipped with wheels or floats, for use as bombers.

The "Ricaurte" was a Curtiss D-12 Falcon used in a flight from the USA to Colombia. It was used for liaison as, despite was the most powerful plane at the beginning, it wasn't armed.

20 Curtiss Model 37F Cyclone Falcon were bought by Colombia as soon as the conflict erupted, for attack missions.

After the conflict, the Cyclone Falcon purchased by Colombia were used mainly on wheels from Palanquero and were painted in silver.

While initially the Cyclone Falcons of Colombia were camouflaged, after the conflict they were painted in silver. For the operations on the Amazon, as well as on the Magdalena River, they used floats.

Three Junkers K43 were purchased by Colombia at the beginning of the conflict and were used as light bombers.

The Junkers W34 purchased by Colombia were used as transports and saw service for a long time after the conflict.

While not used in combat, the Colombian Junkers Ju52/3m were the first of the model used on floats. They were the third, fourth and fifth Ju52/3m built (the first two went to Bolivia).

Three Junkers F13 from SCADTA were sold to the Colombian government and used during the conflict. At least one of them was equipped with a machine gun on the door and they were tested with bombs.

Four Seversky SEV-3M-WW equipped with floats were purchased by Colombia after the conflict and serialled 180 to 183, but their performance was poor due to the resistance caused by the floats and they were retired in 1946.

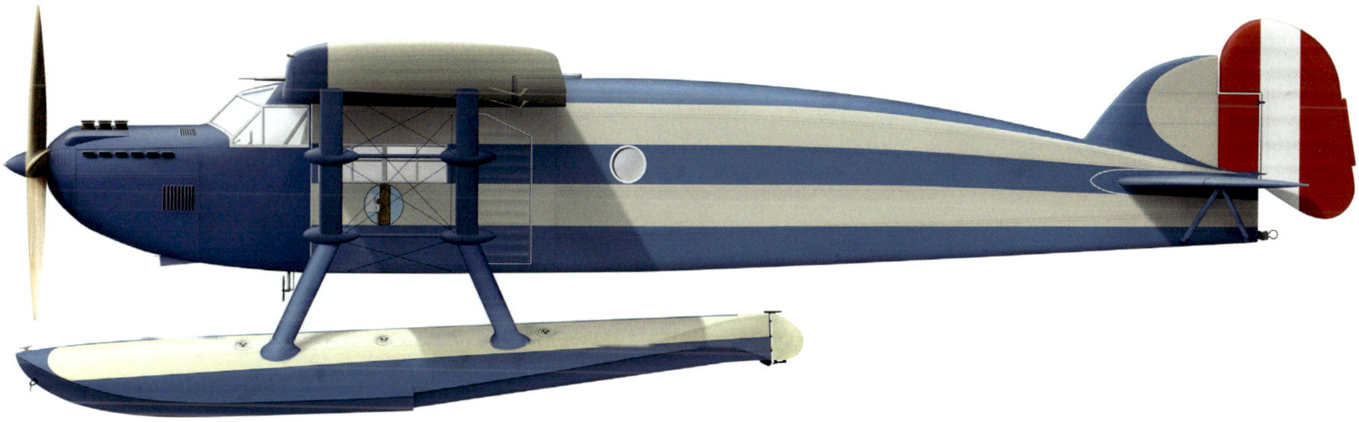

A total of twelve Caproni Ca.111 Idro seaplane bombers were purchased by the Cuerpo de Aviación del Perú from Aeroplani Caproni S.p.A. in April of 1934. To speed deliveries, the aircraft were diverted from Regia Aeronautica stocks.

The Caproni Ca.114 was a biplane fighter developed from the Ca.113 acrobatic airplane during the early thirties. Twelve units were built for the CAP in 1934 and delivered in 1935 along with a single Ca.113 for advanced training.

One of the first purchases made by Peru during the re-equipment process triggered by the September 1932 conflict was a contract for three Curtiss model 35A Hawk II biplane fighters which were delivered in Callao in February 1932.

War is business and the 1932 conflict was no exception for some aviation companies such as the Curtiss-Wright Corporation which sold warplanes to both sides during 1933 and 1934. The CAP took delivery of ten Curtiss model 37F Cyclone Falcon reconnaissance and light attack biplanes in late 1934.

Douglas ½-VG-5 flown by 2nd Lt. Alfredo Rodríguez Ballón was one of the three aircraft formation that arrived at the Nieva River on February 22, 1933, during their ferry flight from Ancón to the operations area. This aircraft and its pilot were lost on that date in an accident during takeoff from that location.

On May 10, 1933 three Douglas O-38P took off from Puca-Barranca with orders to attack Colombian shipping in the Putumayo. Douglas serial ½-VG-4 flown by Lt. Américo Vargas was damaged and had to make an emergency landing over the Algodón River after the formation was surprised by a flight of Colombian Hawk II fighters.

Six Fairey Fox IV, also known as "Peruvian Fox", were purchased by the CAP from the Fairey Aviation Company Limited during the immediate aftermath of the conflict with Colombia. They were delivered with sets of floats and conventional landing gears.

Fairey also managed to obtain an order for six Seal reconnaissance and attack biplanes. These graceful biplanes, equipped with 525hp Armstrong Siddeley Panther IIa radial engines, saw service with the CAP until the mid-forties.

France also provided aircraft during the re-equipment process. After a somewhat tortuous and protracted purchase process a total of 12 exotic Nieuport-Delage NiD-121C.1 parasol fighters were purchased by the CAP.

Other of the obscure types acquired by the CAP during the 1933 rearming process were twelve Potez 390A.2 observation and light attack parasol monoplanes powered by 550hp Lorraine Petrel engines.

In order to cope with the supply demands of the front, the Peruvian government leased a number of Cia de Aviación Faucett S.A. Stinson SM-1 aircraft and their crews. The aircraft were painted in orange to ease their identification in case of accidents.

The only combat capable aircraft in CAP service at the beginning of the conflict were the survivors of a dozen Chance-Vought O2U-1E Corsair biplanes purchased in 1930. However, only five sets of floats were available for them at the start of hostilities.

Corsair serial 5-E-6 was the mount of 2nd Lt. Francisco Secada during the February 14 attack against the "Putumayo expedition" ships moored next to Tarapacá. After facing the intercepting Colombian fighters to allow his comrades escape, he and his gunner managed to evade pursuing Hawk II fighters and return to base unharmed.

Map of Colombia
LEGEND
Colombian Airbases
Colombian River Airbases
Peruvian River Airbases
Colombian Garrisson
Colombian Commanding Post
Peruvian Garrison
Peruvian Commanding Post
Railroad
Horseshoe Path
Footpath
VENEZUELA
COLOMBIA
BRAZIL
ECUADOR
PERU
Riohacha
Santa Marta
Pto. Colombia
Ciénaga
Barranquilla
Cartagena
Sautatá
Cúcuta
Pamplona
Bucaramanga
Barrancabermeja
Cauca R.
Magdalena R.
Utria
Medellín
Sabana
Tunja
Palanquero
Manizales
Palestina
Líbano
Madrid
Bogotá
Techo
Armenia
Ibagué
Girardot
Flandes
Guabito
Buga
Buenaventura
Cali
Santander
Neiva
Guapi
Popayán
Altamira
Garzón
Bolo
Tumaco
Barbacoas
Florencia
Peña Blanca
Venecia
Diviso
Ricaurte
Pasto
Mocoa
Potosí
Ipiales
Tres Esquinas
Pto. Asís
Delícias
Pto. Boy
Pto. Ospina
Isla Chavaco
San Miguel R.
Mondar
Palmar
La Tagua
Güepí
Caucayá
Caquetá R.
Quito
Calamar
Guainía R.
Vaupés R.
Apáporis R.
Putumayo R.
Yubineto R.
Pto. Santander
Caquetá R.
(Cabo) Pantoja
El Encanto
La Chorrera
Pto. Arturo
Napo R.
Campuyá R.
Tambo R.
Ere R.
Igara Paraná R.
Sabaloyacu R.
La Pedrera
Pto. Arica
Putumayo R.
Santa Elena
Algodón R.
Puca Barranca
Putumayo R.
Tarapacá
Buenos Aires
Cotuhé R.
Yaku River Mouth
Pebas
Itaya
Amazonas R.
Amazonas R.
Iquitos
Chimbote
Leticia
Tabatinga
0
100
200 Kilometres
100
200 Miles

Map of Perú
ECUADOR
COLOMBIA
PERU
BRAZIL
QUITO
Riobamba
Guayaquil
Macas
Talara
Pto. Asis
Pto. Boy
Isla Chavaco
Pto. Ospina
San Miguel R.
Güepí
La Tagua
Caucayá
Putumayo R.
Yubineto R.
Caquetá R.
Napo R.
Nashiño
Pantoja
El Encanto
Pto. Arturo
La Chorrera
Pto. Santander
Apáporis R.
La Pedrera
Vila Bittencourt
Campuya R.
Igara Paraná R.
Curaray R.
Napo R.
Ere R.
Sabaloyacu R.
Curaray
Sta. Elena
Pto. Arica
Pucaurco
Putumayo R.
Algodón R.
Puca Barranca
Pastaza R.
Tarapacá
Esperanza
Içá R.
Pebas
Buenos Aires
Cotuhé R.
Yaku River Mouth
Tte. Guillermo Cornejo
Itaya
Iquitos
Amazon R.
Leticia
Tabatinga
Benjamin Constant
Yavari R.
Sta. Maria de Nieva
Marañón R.
Requena
Bellavista
Bayóvar
Ucayali R.
Chachapoyas
8TH Flight Rout to combat theatre
Tarapoto
Chiclayo
Pacasmayo
Cajamarca
Contamana
Cruzeiro do Sul
Huallaga R.
Marañon R.
Virú
Masisea
Chimbote
Tingo María
Ucayali R.
Pto. Inca
Huanuco
Bolognesi
North route to combat theatre
Alto Purus R.
Barranca
Cerro de Pasco
Sotziki
Perené R.
San Ramón
Tambo R.
Mantaro R.
Ancón
Callao
Urubamba R.
Huancayo
Isla San Lorenzo
LIMA
Las Palmas
Manú
LEGEND
Peruvian Airbases
Peruvian River Airbases
Colombian Airbases
Colombian River Airbases
Peruvian Garrison
Peruvian Commanding Post
Colombian Garrisson
Colombian Commanding Post
Railroad
Horseshoe Path
Footpath
Ayacucho
Cusco
Apurimac R.
Pisco
Ica
Nazca
Juliaca
Arequipa
Tarata
Tacna
Arica
0
100
200 Kilometres
100
200 Miles

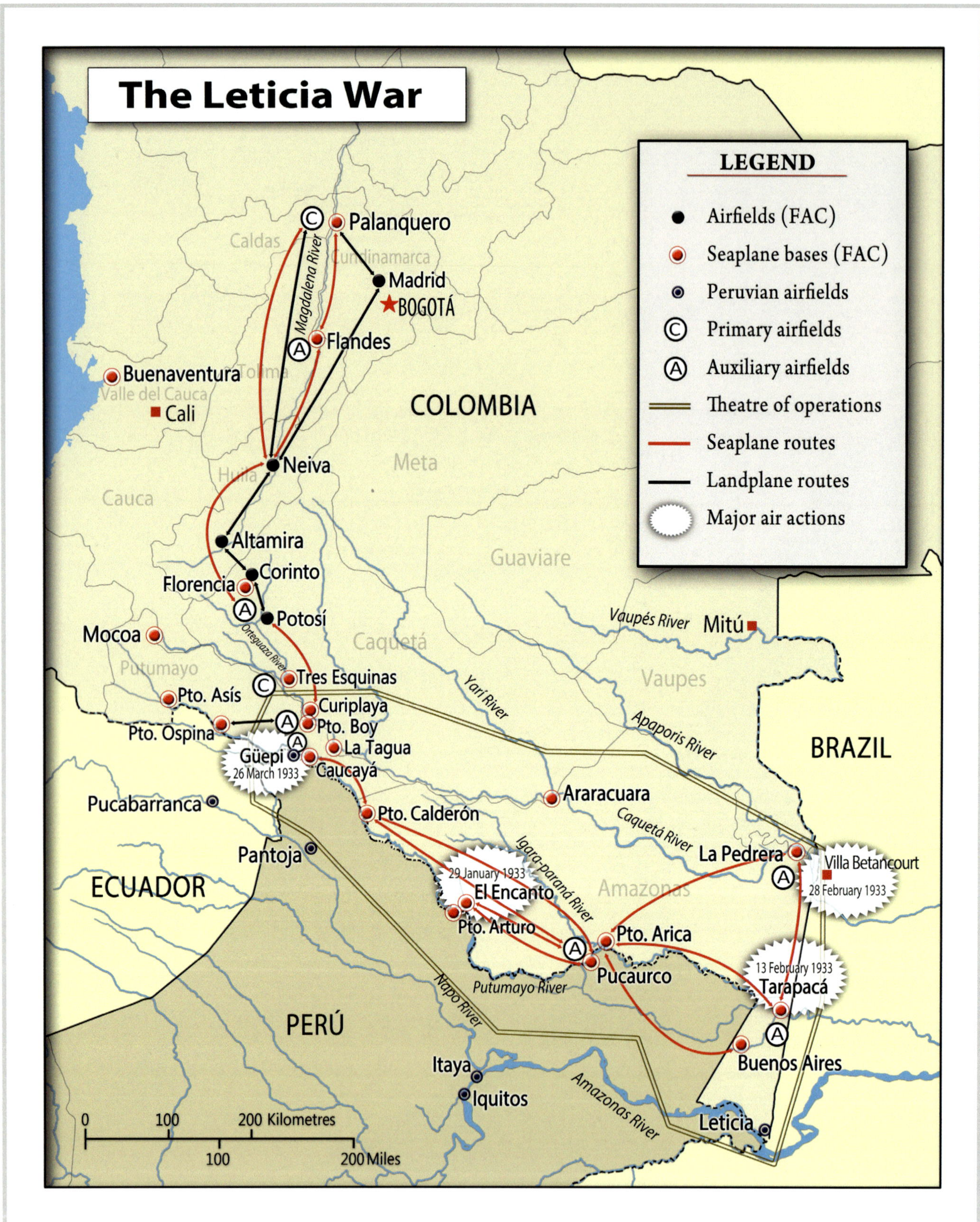
The Leticia War
LEGEND
Airfields (FAC)
Seaplane bases (FAC)
Peruvian airfields
Primary airfields
Auxiliary airfields
Theatre of operations
Seaplane routes
Landplane routes
Major air actions
COLOMBIA
BRAZIL
ECUADOR
PERÚ
Palanquero
Madrid
BOGOTÁ
Flandes
Buenaventura
Cali
Neiva
Altamira
Corinto
Florencia
Potosí
Mocoa
Tres Esquinas
Pto. Asís
Curiplaya
Pto. Boy
Pto. Ospina
La Tagua
Güepi
26 March 1933
Caucayá
Pucabarranca
Pantoja
Pto. Calderón
Araracuara
La Pedrera
Villa Betancourt
28 February 1933
29 January 1933
El Encanto
Pto. Arturo
Pto. Arica
Pucaurco
13 February 1933
Tarapacá
Buenos Aires
Leticia
Itaya
Iquitos
Mitú
Caldas
Cundinamarca
Tolima
Valle del Cauca
Huila
Cauca
Meta
Guaviare
Caquetá
Vaupes
Putumayo
Amazonas
Magdalena River
Ortegueza River
Vaupés River
Yarí River
Apaporis River
Caquetá River
Igara-paraná River
Putumayo River
Napo River
Amazonas River
0
100
200 Kilometres
100
200 Miles

Masisea, October 1932. A pair of Keystones in conventional landing gear configuration seen parked on this connection base which served as an entrance point for the Amazon through the Ucayali River. Archive IEHAP.

where a river fleet of the *Marina de Guerra del Perú* was waiting, led by the *Buque Armada Peruana* (Peruvian Navy Ship – BAP) *America*[19].

On 5 September, the same aircraft took off again on another reconnaissance sortie, this time over the Yavari and Esperanza Rivers in search of the Colombian fleet. On the next day, at 1430hrs, the crew of Keystone serial I-R-1 took off bound for Itaya, carrying urgent correspondence. Three days later, aircraft serial I-R-4 departed Iquitos at 1400hrs towards Puerto Arturo carrying none other than the commissioner for the *Junta Patriotica* – engineer Luis Arana[20] – as well as instructions for the neighbouring garrisons. On 12 October, the LAM was reinforced by the arrival of five aircraft: a CAP Boeing model 40B-2; a Fairchild FC-2W, donated by the Panagra Company; a Bellanca CH-200, donated by civilian pilot Carlos Martinez de Pinillos, as well as a pair of Douglas DT-2B. While the Boeing and the Fairchild were put into good use immediately, the last three machines were in poor condition and, due to their poor performance in height, were scarcely flown during the following months.

Meanwhile, the progressive build-up of combat aircraft on Colombian territory during late October and early November 1932 coincided with the announcement from Bogotá of the launching of the Military Expedition led by General Alfredo Vasquez Cobo and bound for the Putumayo River with the aim of evicting the invading Peruvian forces from Colombian territory. To counter the imminent Colombian offensive, the CAP High Command ordered the reinforcement of its presence in the area, and the available Corsairs were reorganized into the *Quinto Escuadrón de Aviación* (Fifth Aviation Squadron – *V EA*), with two *Escadrilles*, the 8th and 10th of four aircraft each, plus a single Stearman C-3R attached to each fight as hack.

The 8th Flight began its deployment in early November 1932, departing from Las Palmas bound to Sotziki – via San Ramon – where the Corsairs were fitted with floats. Once conversion was completed, the aircraft took off from the Perené River and headed towards Iquitos following the Masisea-Contamana-Requena-Itaya route. Once in Iquitos, the Flight moved on to Pebas, located on the left bank of the Amazon River and about 100km west of Leticia, where the river gunboat BAP *Portillo* and river boats *San Miguel* and *Estefita*, these two adapted as mother ships, awaited their arrival. While the BAP *Portillo* would serve as command post for operations, as it was equipped with a T.S.F.[21] and radio system, both river boats were to provide lodging for the flight crews as well as supplies and maintenance personnel required to keep the aircraft in operation.

After taking up positions around Leticia, the 8th Flight began its first operational missions, which included daily reconnaissance sorties over the Yavari and Amazon rivers, as well as over the mouth of the Putumayo and the Brazilian Amazon, looking for the Colombian fleet. Meanwhile, at Las Palmas, 10th Flight Corsairs were undergoing maintenance whilst waiting for floats and other spare parts. The first days of December saw the 8th Flight still waiting for aviation oil and ammunition supplies to reach adequate levels in order to ensure safe operations, and the command from *V EA* requested the urgent shipment of 7.65mm ammunition and aviation oil from Las Palmas, a request that was only fulfilled ten days later[22]. On 28 December, Commander Montoya took off from Puerto Arturo aboard Keystone I-R-1 with S.O. Vera as mechanic, but upon arrival at Itaya, the aircraft capsized during landing. Fortunately, both crew members were able to escape the wreck unscathed. 8 January 1933 saw the arrival at Callao harbour of the CPV[23] *Ucayali*, which brought six Douglas O-38P purchased in October 1932. After assembly, inspection and

A series of images showing the recovery process of the Keystone serial I-R-1's remains which were performed by the crew of BAP *Napo*. This aircraft had crashed on the Putumayo River on December 27 while returning from a liaison mission to Puerto Arturo. Archivo Histórico de la Marina via Gonzalo Maguiña.

Ten Stearman C-3R arrived in Perú in July of 1930 and were pressed into service in the advanced training and liaison role. At the beginning of the conflict at least three units were fitted with floats. Archive Humberto Currarino.

A ¾ view of a C-3R parked at Las Palmas in the early thirties. Archive Humberto Currarino.

testing, these machines were assigned to the 2nd Information Flight of the newly activated *Primer Escuadrón de Aviación* (First Aviation Squadron – *I EA*). After conversion was completed, the unit flew its aircraft to the seaplane base at Ancon where they were fitted with floats and pilots began their preparations for their imminent deployment to the operations area.

On 23 January 1933, the CAP suffered its first casualties of the campaign at Ancón, as Lt. Humberto Torres was killed aboard Stearman C-3R serial 4-E-1 when it crashed during take-off due to an engine failure. His gunner, Cadet Ernesto Yulo Pardo, was seriously injured and was hospitalized. Operations for January concluded on the 27th with the ferrying of a Travelair S-6000B from Las Palmas to San Ramon airfield. This aircraft was purchased by the Peruvian government through the *Compañia Nacional de Aviacion Faucett S.A.*(Faucett). Meanwhile, the CPV *Urubamba* arrived in Callao carrying the Curtiss model 35A Hawk II acquired by the CAP. The crates were carried to Las Palmas, where they were assembled and tested. After being officially handled over to the CAP, the aircraft were assigned to the 3rd Fighter Flight from *I EA*.

On 5 February, three Douglas took off from Ancon following the Ancon-Bayovar-Santa María de Nieva itinerary, with the leading aircraft being fitted with a radio transmitter in order to allow better coordination between the aviators and the ground posts along the way. The flight remained in Santa María until 9 February, when it took off again bound for Iquitos. During take-off, however, Douglas serial ½-VG-6 hit a log hidden below the surface of the water and capsized. Fortunately, its pilot, Lt. Dañino, escaped without injury. The remaining aircraft completed their journey without incident, reaching Iquitos a few hours later. This accident would mark the beginning of a series of incidents which would affect CAP units during February. Two days later, Corsair serial 2-E-3 flown by Captain Valderrama crashed during take-off from Pebas. In this case the pilot was also able to walk away from the wreck, suffering only a few bruises. The aircraft, however, was a total loss.

Tension leads to fight

While Peru decided to reinforce their positions all along the border with Colombia, including the occupied towns of Leticia and Tarapacá, Colombia decided to act and try to recover the lost territory. Two lines of approach were determined, one being the *Expedición Punitiva* across the Amazon, to attack Tarapacá, and the other was from the west, with Caucayá as the main base of operations, to gain control of the whole Putumayo River which was the border with Peru. The Colombian plan included, after that, to take Leticia and then, a direct attack against Iquitos, as this was the main Peruvian city on the Amazon. Instead, General Vázquez Cobo preferred to attack Leticia before Tarapacá.

As the Colombian riverine fleet was sailing through the Amazon River, on 13 January Junkers 202 was sent to Manaus, with Herbert Boy at the controls. This carried Colonel Acevedo to meet Generals Vázquez Cobo and Efráin Rojas, in command of the small fleet, with the order from the government that they should attack Tarapacá instead of Leticia. The latter place was well defended by the Peruvian riverine fleet and the Peruvian position at Ramón Castilla, in front of Leticia, could fire on the boats too, putting them into a crossfire. They took off from Puerto Boy and made a first stop at La Pedrera and, with the support of another F13, they sent fuel to an island on the Caquetá River – inside Brazilian territory – to facilitate a stop there on their return, as the distance between La Pedrera and Manaus was 1,100km. To find the island from the air, they put a white sheet over the trees. After the meeting of Colonel Acevedo and Boy with the generals, they returned to Bogotá to inform the Army command, completing the trip in two days.

On 29 January 1933, the position at Caucayá received an urgent message from El Encanto, informing them that they had been attacked, but the transmission was cut short and they couldn't get any further information. A plane was immediately sent with Herbert Boy, a mechanic, and doctor Patiño Camargo, to evacuate possible casualties. Once at El Encanto they found that a patrol had been attacked by Peruvian forces and soldier Cándido Leguízamo was severely wounded. They prepared a stretcher during the night and on the following day he was evacuated to Caucayá, and from there to Bogotá, but he died some time later.

Meanwhile, as the planes at Caucayá, stationed on the river that formed the border with Peru, were exposed to enemy fire from the southern coast of the river, a new base was built some kilometres to the north of La Tagua on the Caquetá River. This was named Puerto Boy, in honour to Herbert Boy, and was transformed into the main airfield for operations on the Amazon. During January, the Junkers F13 202 was used by Captain von Engel and Lieutenant José Ignacio Forero (both being SCADTA pilots who received military rank during operations) for many flights to carry supplies from Potosí to Puerto Boy, as the river was very low and prevented the ship with supplies from arriving.

On 8 February, the Colombian aviation suffered another loss when Lieutenant Guillermo Zornosa Sanchez crashed in Flandes, aboard a Curtiss Osprey, when he was taking off towards La Tagua.

A C-3R assigned to the Escuadrilla de Transportes takes off from Piura forward airfield during the Summer of 1932. This unit provided transport services across the Peruvian coastal areas. Archive Humberto Currarino.

Picture of Puerto Boy, one of the Colombian bases created during the conflict and named after SCADTA pilot Herbert Boy

In the meantime, to support the attack on Tarapacá, the Colombian military aviation was prepared at Puerto Boy and, by 10 February, four of the new Curtiss Hawk, the Junkers K43 serialled 402, and the F13 serialled 203, acting as bombers, were deployed to the Putumayo River, where the ships were anchored inside Brazilian territory, supported by some Junkers transports which were deployed to La Pedrera. The Colombian government had received permission from Brazil to deploy up to six planes to protect the ships, and the first three planes arrived at Tomantins, in Brazil, on 13 February.

The attack on Tarapacá was to be carried out by the gunboats *Córdova* and *Barranquilla* landing troops of the second fusilier company, and the machinegun section, downriver following a bombardment with artillery, with the *Pichincha* and *Nariño* as a reserve – with a company of infantry. The *Mosquera* and *Boyacá* moved to São Paulo de Olivença on the Amazon, a one-day trip from Leticia, to make the Peruvians think they would move to attack Leticia at the same time. The plan included a follow-up advance against Leticia, with troops moving from Tarapacá while the boats sailed back through the Putumayo and then up the Amazon river. An attack would then be made by the *Destacamento Putumayo* against the Peruvian town of Güeppi and from there move by land to Pantoja on the upper part of the Napo River, to threaten Peruvian communications, while the *Destacamento Amazonas* would move to the mouth of the Napo, close to the city of Iquitos. The last action planned was the attack against Iquitos, with the aim of reaching a final victory.

On 11 February, the Peruvian Vought Corsairs 5-E-6 and 2-E-4 flown by Cmdr. Montoya and 2nd Lt. Gal'Lino, respectively, took off from their base at the Yacu River mouth bound for Tarapacá on a reconnaissance mission. Once over their objective, the pilots spotted the Colombian *Expedición Punitiva* moored in Brazilian waters of the Putumayo River and, after orbiting for a while, the crews returned to base to report the sighting. With the news of the Colombian expedition's arrival, the *V EA* command ordered an attack to be carried against the fleet the next day.

Consequently, according to Peruvian sources, shortly after noon on 12 February, a formation from 8th Flight composed of the Corsairs 2-E-4, 5-E-2, 5-E-6 and 5-E-7, each armed with eight 15kg bombs, and flown by Cmdr. Montoya, Captain Pedro Canga, 2nd Lt. Francisco Secada and Lt. Arturo Lecca, respectively, took off to attack the Colombian fleet, which was now anchored near the Brazilian town of Ipiranga, at only one kilometre from the border with Colombia. Arriving over their objective with the sun on their backs, the formation surprised the Colombian defenders who were unable to prevent the attack nor to intercept the planes on their escape. However, despite having the element of surprise, the Peruvian attack failed to achieve the intended results, mostly due to the fact that their bombs did not explode upon scoring either direct hits or near misses on the Colombian ships. This action does not appear in the Colombian records, which only include a reconnaissance mission by Peruvian planes on midday of the 13th, but without mention of any attack upon their ships.

Operations by the Peruvians resumed on the morning of 13 February, with a supply mission flown by Lt. Elias Moreno, who took off from Itaya aboard Stearman serial 4-E-3 carrying a radio and medical supplies destined for the Peruvian garrison of Güeppi. Escorting the Stearman was the Vought Corsair serial 5-E-8 flown by 2nd Lt. Humberto Gal'Lino. Once the supplies had been delivered, both aircraft began their return to Itaya, but as they started their take-off run they came under attack from small arms fired from Colombian positions located on the opposite side of the river, and both aircraft sustained hits. While Lt. Moreno was able to take off, Gal'Lino's Corsair received several hits in its lateral fuel tanks, bursting into flames and prompting its pilot and gunner to abandon the aircraft, suffering only minor burns.

Chapter 8
COMBAT OPERATIONS

In action over Tarapacá

After the six Colombian planes joined the small fleet by the end of 13 February, at 0800hrs of the 14th, a formation of four Peruvian Corsairs took off from the Yacu (Napo) River mouth and headed to Tarapacá, seeking to repeat the surprise achieved on the 12th. Their luck, however, abandoned them shortly after take-off as one of the Corsairs had to return to base due to an engine malfunction. The group continued towards their target and once over Tarapacá they found more bad news, as they were intercepted by a flight of Hawk II fighters, which had managed to take off as soon as they spotted the Voughts. Without fighter escort, the chances of success for the Peruvian attack were slim at best and, therefore, the formation leader ordered the bombs to be dropped and a return to base. The Colombian fighters were, however, already too close and gave chase to the intruders. According to the Colombian sources, the planes attacked the *Córdova*, which was anchored separate from the rest, but there were no bomb hits.

One of the two Do J II Wals ordered by the Colombian Air Arm and received in December 1933. Archive Javier Franco.

One of the Wals purchased newly built serving at Palanaquero with camouflage paint. They were used both over the ocean and over the rivers. Archive Javier Franco.

A Do J II Wal at the Magdalena River in front of Palanquero Air Base. Archive Javier Franco.

A sizeable quantity of Curtiss model 37F Cyclone Falcon were ordered by Colombian military aviation in 1932. This model 37F was seen parked at the Curtiss-Wright Airplane Co. factory in St Louis, Missouri, shortly before delivery in October of 1932. Note the .30 cal machine gun bulges on top of the lower wings. Archive Dan Hagedorn.

What happened next, according to Peruvian accounts, is that 2nd Lt. Francisco Secada, flying Corsair 5-E-6, broke formation and maneuvered into a head-on attack against the Hawks and passed through them with his machine guns blazing, breaking the enemy attack and attracting the attention of the Colombian pilots and, thus, allowing the remaining Corsairs to escape unharmed. During the uneven combat that followed, which lasted for more than ten minutes, Secada maneuvered his Corsair to the limits while his gunner – S.O. Mario Dolci – made good use of his Browning machine gun in the rear position Scarff ring, managing to evade the Colombian fire. Unable to keep up with the nimbler Corsair, the Colombian pilots gave up and abandoned the hunt, returning to Tarapacá. In his book, Herbert Boy says that the only Hawk to take off was his, and that his machine guns jammed[24].

The combat between Secada and the Colombian Hawk IIs served to confirm to the CAP the results of the evaluations held at Ancon after the arrival of the Hawk II ordered by Peru. These results stated

On October of 1932 Curtiss also sold 26 Curtiss model 35 Hawk II fitted with 600hp Wright SR-1820F-2 Cyclone engines to the Colombian military aviation. The first deliveries of these aircraft took place later that very same year. Archive Richard Dann.

Line of Colombian Curtiss Model 37F Cyclone Falcon seen after the conflict.

This beautiful picture shows a camouflaged Colombian Curtiss Model 37F Cyclone Falcon flying low over the Amazon forest landscape. Photo Col. Jesse Rothrock.

that the performance of the Curtiss fighter dropped heavily when floats were fitted, turning it into a sluggish machine unable to dogfight with more agile adversaries. Therefore, a slower but more agile target such as the Corsair had chances to evade attack without much effort after dropping its bomb load.

On that afternoon, the Colombians ordered the bombing of the Peruvian forces at Tarapacá by the Junkers, with Colonel Acevedo dropping light bombs from the opening in the floor and manning a machine gun in one of the windows to strafe the enemy troops. At the same time, the ships crossed the border and entered Colombian waters, preparing the assault for the next morning. During the early hours of the following day, the Peruvian Army garrison, seeing that they would be assaulted by troops from the ships and facing numerically superior forces evacuated their defensive positions, using the launch *Estefita,* through the Cotuhe River and then through the jungle towards the Amazon River. Boy insisted on attacking the vessel, but General Vázquez Cobo would not authorize that. At sunset, a reconnaissance made by the aviation indicated the position was abandoned, but nevertheless, on the following day, the Colombians landed and occupied Tarapacá. The gunboats fired against the positions and the airplanes strafed them, but there was no resistance; the position had been deserted and the troops captured only ammunition and an old artillery piece left behind by the retreating forces. The two Junkers

One of the two Do J II Wals just after its arrival. Archive Javier Franco.

One of the Consolidated P2Y-1C flying boat seen after the conflict, with a new paint scheme.

Colombia also purchased two Consolidated P2Y-1C flying boat in early December 1932 with the aim to employ it as a long-range reconnaissance bomber. The aircraft, delivered in aluminium finish, was promptly painted dark green shortly after its arrival later that very same month. Archive Dan Hagedorn.

were deployed with Captains Gómez Niño and Lt. Forero as pilots of the K43 and F13 respectively.

At the same time as the occupation of Tarapacá, on the 14th, diplomatic relations between Peru and Colombia were broken off with the withdrawal of their ambassadors from each other's capital cities. Meanwhile, on that same day, another accident resulted in human and material losses. While taking off from Barrancabermeja aboard a Hawk II, Captain Helmuth Breitfeld struck a trunk covered

Colombia also ordered large quantities of Curtiss model 35A Hawk II biplane fighters, most of which were delivered before the end of the conflict and deployed to the Putumayo. They were fitted with EDO floats which allowed water operations but also heavily restricted the Hawk´s famous manoeuvrability. Archive Dan Hagedorn.

by water, and invisible to him, causing the overturning of his aircraft; destroying it and losing his life in the process.

The CAP attacks reassumed on 16 February when the whole 8th Flight was sent to attack Colombian ground positions, and the fleet moored in the proximity of Tarapacá. The four planes attacked the *Barranquilla*, which was upriver, searching for possible Peruvian forces. Again, Colombian fighters were on alert and two of them appeared to counter the attack force, but the Peruvians pressed their attack, with the Corsair gunners' fierce defensive fire managing to keep the Colombians at bay. It is worth mentioning that, after returning to base, the Peruvian crews issued complains regarding the effectiveness of the 15 and 25kg bombs as, similar to the previous attack, they failed to explode.

After the recovery of Tarapacá, the Hawks and the Junkers were based there for some days, in order to protect the town and the gunboats, until they received the order to return to Puerto Boy on 28 February. The Junkers F13 had to make an emergency landing near the Brazilian outpost of Villa Betancourt, on the border with Colombia, when it ran out of fuel. A day later the fuel was delivered by the other Junkers and both arrived at Puerto Boy.

On 19 February, the Peruvian Corsair 5-E-7, flown by Cmdr. Canepa, left Ancon bound for Itaya to replace the machine lost in Güeppi on 13 February. This aircraft, however, never arrived at its destination as it plunged to the ground on a beach at Viru, due to an engine malfunction, killing its crew. Three days later, the remaining O-38Ps were transferred to the front line, again following the northern route and the Nieva River, making a refuelling stop for the formation, where there was another incident, this time with tragic consequences. Douglas ½-VG-5 flown by 2nd Lt. Alfredo Rodriguez Ballon lost power as it was taking off causing the aircraft to crash against the surface, killing its pilot and severely wounding his gunner, S.O. Oscar Espejo. Later, investigations showed that the poor quality of the fuel was the cause of the engine malfunction that led to the catastrophe[25].

After the loss of Tarapacá, the *V EA* reoriented its efforts to the defence of the Güeppi garrison, which was under direct threat from the Colombians advancing upriver. The mission carried out on 22 February was of particular importance, when a mixed formation of Vought and Douglas aircraft – composed of Corsairs serialled 5-E-5, 5-E-4 and 5-E-6, as well as Douglas O-38P serialled ½-VG-2 and ½-VG-4 – took off from their provisional bases in Santa Isabel and Callaru, heading for the Putumayo to look for the Colombian troop transport *Pichincha*, which had been sighted in the proximity of the River Cotuhe, 10 km north east of Tarapacá. Arriving over Tarapacá,

Palanquero airbase, November of 1932. Several Colombian aircraft, including a Curtiss model 35A Hawk II, a camouflaged Dornier Wal and a Junkers Ju 52/3m, can be seen in this picture taken on this former SCADTA base, strategically located on the bank of the Magdalena River.

The Curtiss Model 35A Hawk II were purchased by Colombia for the conflict and were the main fighters of the force in the '30s.

A camouflaged Junkers K43 of the Colombian Air Arm in 1933.

The Colombians built several mock planes on their bases in the Putumayo region to confuse the Peruvians.

the formation spotted several enemy ships, protected by aviation, and pressed on the attack being welcomed by anti-aircraft fire. One of the aircraft, nonetheless, managed to score a hit on the *Pichincha,* albeit without causing much damage. The fight, however, was not one-sided as four of the attacking aircraft received hits from both AA and the Hawks. As consequence, Lt. Ismael Merino and S.O. Mario Dolci, pilot and gunner from Douglas ½-VG-2 and Vought 5-E-6, respectively, sustained minor wounds.

By the end of February, and as a consequence of the poor results displayed by locally manufactured explosives, the Peruvian Navy ordered 700 aviation bombs from France, with deliveries expected a month later. On the 1 March, the CAP signed a contract with Faucett

One of the Colombian Junkers K43 on a river on the Amazon region.

A Curtiss Falcon of the Colombian Air Arm on the bank of a river in the Putumayo region, with the camouflage applied for the conflict.

View of Palanquero Air Base in 1933, with the Curtiss Osprey in front, a Junkers K43 and two Curtiss Hawk in the background. Photo Col. Jesse Rothrock.

Colombian Curtiss Hawks, Falcons and other planes in line at Palanquero in 1933. Photo Col. Jesse Rothrock.

for the lease, for a period of one-month-and-five-days, of a Stinson SM-1D aircraft to be employed on transport duties between Las Palmas and San Ramón. With the pace of operations scaling up, the CAP's attrition ratio also began to mount. In Ancón on 8 March 1933, Cadet Bolaños crashed into the sea while taking off aboard a Boeing model 40B-2 due to lack of experience on the type. Fortunately, the pilot was able to escape from the wreck only with minor injuries.

On 16 March, the CAP began the transfer, via the centre route, of the trio of Hawk II fighters recently arrived in the country. The aircraft were identified by CAP serials ½-VF-1 to ½-VF-3. Once at Sotziki the aircraft received floats with the help of the CAP personnel deployed to that location and, immediately after, were taken to the Perené River from where they took off bound for the theatre of operations. However, once again the lack of experience on the type caused an incident as Captain César Álvarez Guerra crashed aboard

A pilot and mechanics with a Colombian Curtiss Falcon at Tarapacá during the conflict. Photo Col. Jesse Rothrock.

A Colombian Curtiss Falcon seen at La Tagua, on the Caquetá River. Photo Col. Jesse Rothrock.

Colombian Lt. "Pepi" Cajio in front of a Curtiss Falcon at Tarapacá. Photo Col. Jesse Rothrock.

A Colombian Curtiss Falcon flies over the Amazon. Note that, as usual when they first arrived in Columbia, this plane is not wearing camouflage. Photo Col. Jesse Rothrock.

A Colombian Curtiss Falcon on a river near the area of Leticia in times of the conflict. Photo Col. Jesse Rothrock.

A Colombian Curtiss Falcon flying over the Caquetá River, on the Amazon region. Photo Col. Jesse Rothrock.

the Hawk serialled ½-V-F-3 during take-off, damaging a float and the propeller in the process. With one aircraft fewer, the formation continued north, reaching the forward base in the mouth of the Yacu River a few hours later.

The day after their arrival, the fighters took part in their first combat mission, escorting three Voughts and three Douglas' during a bombing mission against Colombian forces attacking Peruvian Army units at the garrison of Tambo de Hilario, located on the bank of the Cotuhe River. The urgency of this operation, ordered by the command, meant that the aircraft had to depart from their base at

A non-camouflaged Curtiss Falcon of the Colombian Air Arm flying over the Caquetá River. Photo Col. Jesse Rothrock.

A Colombian Falcon without camouflage flying over the Amazon. Photo Col. Jesse Rothrock.

Colombian Curtiss Falcon serialled 111 over the Putumayo River. Photo Col. Jesse Rothrock.

The Curtiss Falcon was the main attack plane of the Colombians, purchased during the conflict. Before that, only the Junkers F13, modified locally to carry machine guns and bombs, had any attack capacity. Photo Col. Jesse Rothrock.

A Colombian Curtiss Cyclone Falcon flying over the Caquetá River. Photo Col. Jesse Rothrock.

A Colombian Curtiss Cyclone Falcon and its pilot at Potosí. Photo Col. Jesse Rothrock.

One Colombian Curtiss Falcon operating at La Tagua. Photo Col. Jesse Rothrock.

A Colombian Curtiss Falcon on the Magdalena River at Neiva. Photo Col. Jesse Rothrock.

A Colombian Curtiss Falcon at La Tagua. This small town, on the Caquetá River, was used to help ferry troops and supplies from the city of Florencia. From La Tagua, they were taken by land to Caucayá. Photo Col. Jesse Rothrock.

1700hrs, arriving over the target after almost an hour of flight. Once over Tambo de Hilario, the formation carried out their attack in almost darkness, dropping a total of 540kg of explosives on a vessel, as well as on Colombian positions located nearby, causing the vessel to

The small town of Venecia, close to the city of Florencia, was one of the places from where all the supplies were taken by the Caquetá River to La Tagua or La Pedrera, for the operations on the Putumayo.

The Colombian Navy boat *Nariño* and a Curtiss Falcon operating near Leticia. Photo Col. Jesse Rothrock.

A Colombian Curtiss Cyclone Falcon in operations at the Putumayo region during the conflict. Photo Col. Jesse Rothrock.

retreat downriver to reach safety.

At 0500hrs on 20 March, the Colombian ships besieging Güeppi were attacked by three Corsairs and four O-38P from 8th and 10th Flights, respectively, escorted by two Hawk IIs from 3rd Flight. According to Peruvian documents, during the Peruvian attack the Colombian aviators refused to engage in aerial combat, retreating

The Colombian Navy vessels *Boyacá, Córdova, Pichincha* and *Mosquera* on the Amazon while being deployed to retake Tarapacá.

Crew of the Colombian Air Arm with a Junkers K43 at La Tagua. Photo Col. Jesse Rothrock.

Port of La Tagua, with a sign indicating "Aircraft Port", and a Junkers K43 in the background. Photo Col. Jesse Rothrock.

towards their own airspace.

On 22 March, a formation of CAP aircraft composed of Corsair 2-E-1 flown by Lt. Alvariño Herr, accompanied by 1st NCO S.O. Hector Rubio Cavassa, a Stinson SM-1, flown by civilian pilot Mr. Dan E. Tobin, and a Keystone K-55, flown by and Lt. Chirinos, took off from San Ramón bound for Masisea carrying supplies to the operations area. While en route, however, the formation found bad weather which led Lt. Alvariño, the flight leader, to order Mr. Tobin and Lt. Chirinos to return to San Ramón as he, confident in his flying abilities and given the urgency of his cargo, carried on towards Masisea[26]. Their aircraft, however never reached its destination and the crew was declared as missing.

On 23 March, new aircraft arrived at Las Palmas in the form of a single Curtiss P-1 Hawk and two Curtiss O-1E Falcon. These aircraft were purchased by the Peruvian Ambassador in Santiago, for a total amount of 223,776 Soles, a beefy amount of money for the time. The acquisition was a clear breach of CAP purchasing regulations, not only because of the fact that the D-12 engine which powered all three machines was not standard equipment used by the CAP, but also because the afore mentioned aircraft arrived devoid of any kind of armament. For these reasons, CAP High Command decided to keep the machines at Las Palmas, assigning them to the *Escuela de Aviacion Militar* (Military Aviation School, EAM) where they were pressed into service as trainers.

The Colombian assault against the Güeppi garrison began on 26 March, supported by eleven Colombian aircraft and 600 troops from the "*Destacamento Putumayo*". The besieged EP forces fought for eight hours against the Colombian onslaught from their elaborate defensive positions, but low morale and Colombian numerical superiority forced the Peruvians to abandon them, leaving behind much equipment which could not be evacuated in time (including the wreck of Corsair 5-E-8).

The fight for Güeppi

Despite the plan to attack Leticia, it was decided to wait for the arrival of the ships *Bogotá* and *Mariscal Sucre* and the increase in the level of the Amazon in March, as the town of Ramón Castilla would be flooded. This delay, and the control of the lower Putumayo River lead to a change of plans, with a focus on controlling the river.

There were two important Peruvian positions on the river; Güeppi on the upper part of the river, a few kilometres from the border between

Colombian Curtiss Falcon serialled 114 at La Tagua. Photo Col. Jesse Rothrock.

One of the first three Junkers Ju52/3m at Puerto Boy. Note the ventral fairing for the gunner position. Photo Col. Jesse Rothrock.

A Colombian Falcon lands at Cali. Photo Col. Jesse Rothrock.

Peru and Ecuador, and Puerto Arturo, on the middle. The Colombian forces finally decided to attack Güeppi, to expel the Peruvians from the upper Putumayo River, as it was less well defended than Puerto Arturo and the operation could be made by the *Destacamento Putumayo*, while the *Destacamento Amazonas* was threatening Puerto Arturo by performing a reconnaissance of the lower Putumayo, to the west of Tarapacá. The attack would be carried out with a landing from the boats of the *Flotilla del Amazonas*, supporting the infantry with their guns, and with an air strike from the plane operating from Puerto Boy.

Initially it was planned for mid-February, but progress on the peace negotiations in Geneva led to a delay on the actions and, by early March, the troops deployed to the position of Chavaco, close to Güeppi, on the Colombian shore of the Putumayo, were taken back to Caucayá. After a recommendation by the League of Nations that the Peruvians should leave Leticia, which was rejected by the Peru, on 18 March the Colombian War Minister informed the forces of the *Destacamento Putumayo* to proceed with the attack against Güeppi.

With the start of the assault on Güeppi, the gunboats *Cartagena* and *Santa Marta* of the *Flotilla del Putumayo*, plus some towed barges and small motor boats approached the position, carrying only part of the six hundred troops under Colonel Roberto D. Rico, as there was not enough space on the vessels to carry all of them in one trip. They also carried two 75mm guns and a section of machine guns. As air cover, the Colombian forces had six Hawk II and six Curtiss Cyclone Falcon, half of them for the initial attack and the others to relive them over the target.

Two Junkers Ju52/3m at Palanquero. They arrived by the end of the conflict and saw no action, despite the first three being able to be used as bombers. Photo Col. Jesse Rothrock.

Junkers Ju52/3m serialled 622 and a Junkers K43 at Puerto Boy. Photo Col. Jesse Rothrock.

On 25 March 1933, the *Cartagena* sailed to the west of Güeppi behind two small islands that covered its movement from the Peruvians. Those islands were occupied by the machine guns section in order to fire against the Peruvians. In the early hours of the 26th, troops from the *Cartagena* landed to the west of Güeppi, on what is now Ecuadorian territory, and moved towards the Peruvian position.

Hangars at Palanquero, with a Curtiss Hawk and a Cyclone Falcon (serial 113) clearly visible. Photo Gumersindo Cuellar.

Hangar at Palanquero, with one Hawk on wheels, two on floats, two Cyclone Falcon and one Osprey on floats. Pictures of the Osprey with floats are very rare, while this airplane is also wearing camouflage. The two Falcons and one of the Hawks are painted on metal finish. Photo Gumersindo Cuellar.

Colombian Curtiss Hawk serial 807, with the camouflage used during the war.

Meanwhile, more troops landed to the east of Güeppi, from the *Santa Marta*, and approached from that direction to cut the track that ran from Güeppi to the town of Pantoja in the south. The two field guns were positioned on the Colombian side of the river, at Chavaco.

The Peruvian Army had an infantry company and machine gun company at Güeppi, and they already had detected the occupation of the two islands in front of them on 11 February, but the reinforcement of the position was only ordered on 22 March, moving the *Batallón de Infantería de Montaña No.27* from Iquitos to Pantoja and from there to Güeppi, but it was too late.

The attack began at 0840hrs on the 26th, with the aircraft coming from Puerto Boy and strafing and bombing the ground positions of the Peruvians, staying over Güeppi until the infantry initiated their assault. The Curtiss Hawk IIs of Captains von Ortzen and von Engel suffered hits from the Peruvian anti-aircraft artillery that caused minor damage to their aircraft. At the same time, the field artillery, the guns from the gunboats and the machine guns on the islands opened fire against the Peruvian positions. The attack by the airplanes served as a distraction for the approach of the infantry, who attacked the Bolognesi trenches from the east, while the forces from the west crossed the Güeppi river on small boats, covered by the fire of the *Cartagena*. The *Santa Marta*, together with some small boats, landed the remainder of the battalion.

The infantry surrounded the Peruvians and assaulted the positions, supported by continuous artillery fire. After some fighting, they forced the Peruvian garrison to retreat to the town of Pantoja at midday, while a group of 39 men, including 14 wounded, was captured. 27 Peruvians and 16 Colombians had died during the action. At 3:00 p.m. a group of about 80 Peruvians attempted a counterattack, but they were repelled and then retreated to Tambo Zuñiga on the track

View of the town of Güeppi, captured by the Colombians.

A Vought which had just returned from a mission over the Putumayo is serviced by ground personnel in order to prepare it for the next mission.

Keyston K-55 and a Boeing model 40B-2 seen at Pucallpa airfield in late 1933. Archive Amaru Tincopa.

A rare aerial view of Boeing model 40B-2 assigned to the *Primer Escuadron de Transporte Pesado* from *IV Escuadron de Aviacion* during 1934. Archive IEHAP

to Pantoja.

On the following day, the first group of reinforcements coming from Iquitos arrived, and all attempted to move to Güeppi, but again were repelled by the Colombians, who had improved their positions.

After the loss of Güeppi, the Peruvian V Division prepared a counter-offensive, and ordered CAP units to attack Colombian river traffic around the garrison, with the aim of cutting the flow of supplies to Colombian forces in the garrison so as to debilitate them. In order to accomplish these objectives, the *10th Escadrille* moved its operations to a forward base in Puca-Barranca, a populated centre located on the Napo River, from which the Peruvian aircraft could cover the whole Putumayo River. Operations reassumed on 28 March when four Voughts headed north west to attack Colombian fluvial shipping in the vicinity of Güeppi. During the take-off, however, the Corsair serialled 5-E-4 flown by 2nd Lt. Morante crashed after hitting a log hidden underwater. Luckily for the crew, the bomb load did not detonate with the crash and both pilot and gunner were able to leave the wreck with only bruises. Meanwhile, the rest of the formation continued towards their objective, and once arriving over Güeppi the gunboat *Santa Marta* was sighted and attacked with bombs and machine gun fire, with a bomb exploding very close. Immediately after they saw the launches *Emmita* and *Sinchi Roca* which were carrying the prisoners and wounded. The crew of the *Sinchi Roca* beached the boat and all escaped before she was hit, but the pilot was killed. The aircraft returned to Puca-Barranca where they reported good results. The next day, the unit began to carry out reconnaissance sorties over the Algodón, Putumayo, Igaraparana, Ere, Yubinete, Campuya and Sabaloyacu rivers, looking for any signs of Colombian shipping, following the orders from V Division command. However, the loss of two Voughts during the previous days, as well as an experienced pilot such as Alvariño, were a hard blow to CAP operations in the area and further aggravated the precarious CAP combat aircraft availability situation in the Putumayo. In order to ensure the effective execution of the assigned tasks the *10th Escadrille* strength was reinforced with

After rearming the aircraft with bombs and ammunition, the ground crews cover the engine of the Corsair leaving it ready for another mission once the order arrives. Note the presence of MGP support vessel Emmita on the right. Archive Humberto Currarino.

A view of Vought 5-E-6 moored on the bank of the Yubinete river, in the Amazon forest.

Corsair 5-E-5 seen moored at Puca-Barranca during a pause in operations. This aircraft was heavily damaged after being hit by Colombian fire during a liaison sortie to Güepí. Archive IEHAP.

Vought Corsairs serials 2-E-4 and 5-E-2 wait for the beginning of another sortie at Puca-Barranca base, March of 1933. Archive Humberto Currarino.

Vought Corsairs serials 5-E-2 and 5-E-6 moored at Puca-Barranca in between operations during May of 1933. Archive IEHAP.

A Beautiful shot of Vought serial 2-E-4 at Puca-Barranca in March of 1933. This strategic Peruvian base was located approximately 100km north west of Iquitos, in the heart of the Amazon. From this location the Peruvian aircraft could cover both the eastern and western Putumayo river. Archive IEHAP.

Pebas, 11 February 1933. The wreck of Capt. Valderrama's Vought Corsair after it flipped over during take-off. when its main float hit a hidden log during take-off. Fortunately for the crew, despite the heavy impact the bombs hanging on the bomb racks didn't explode. Archive IEHAP.

A pair of Curtiss O-1E equipped with D-12 engines were purchased by the Peruvian Ambassador in Chile to the representative of Curtiss Airplane and Motor Co. at Santiago. Both planes were delivered without machine guns and bomb racks, so they were used for training. Archive IEHAP.

The crew of 1/2-VG-1 pose for the cameraman shortly after returning from another mission over the Putumayo river in April of 1933. Archive Humberto Currarino.

the aircraft from 8th *Escadrille*. Similar sorties were launched on a daily basis until 12 April.

Ground clashes continued in the vicinity of Güeppi, with the 23rd and 27th Infantry Battalions of the Peruvian Army occupying Pantoja and sending patrols and small forces to harass the vanguard of the Colombian positions.

Meanwhile, in Lima, the reception of flying material continued. On 16 April, a Ford 4-AT Tri-motor transport arrived at Las Palmas. This aircraft was purchased second hand in the US via Harold B. Grow – former Director of the Peruvian Naval Aviation Service, now turned into an arms dealer – at a cost of $10,000 USD. As there was not a single landing strip long enough to allow this aircraft safe operation in the mountains, the Ford was assigned to transport duties along the coast.

On 20 April, the Peruvian 2nd Observation Flight sent its O-38Ps from Puca-Barranca on an armed reconnaissance sortie over the Yubinete river mouth, where they discovered and attacked the

CAP flying personnel stand on top of the starboard float from O-38P serial ½-VG2 stationed at Puca-Barranca in late March of 1933. Archive Humberto Currarino.

Members from the *Escuadrilla Mixta* portrayed next to one of the O-38P from the unit. Archive IEHAP.

A rare image showing the aircraft ½-VG-4 flown by Capt. Vargas during the beginning of its take-off run from Puca-Barranca on May 10, 1933. The aircraft was part of a formation heading to the Putumayo with the mission to attack Colombian shipping. Archive IEHAP.

transport *Emmita*. A similar sortie was flown on 22 April, this time the *Sinchi Roca* was the subject of the Douglas´ attention. Meanwhile in

Curtiss model 35A and Douglas O-38P aircraft seen stationed at Puca-Barranca in early May of 1933. Archive IEHAP.

Hamilton H-45 serial I-R-10 seen on the waters of Itaya river shortly before starting its take-off run on a liaison mission over the Amazon.

The sun sets in the Amazon while an O-38P rest moored at the Yacu River mouth forward base. Archive Humberto Currarino.

With the CAP reorganization launched in June of 1933 the H-45 serial I-R-10 became T-051. Archive Humberto Currarino.

The CAP took delivery of a second H-45 in the summer of 1933. Both Hamiltons served with the *Transport Escadrille* and then the *V Escuadrón de Aviación* with home base in Itaya. Archive Roberto Gentili.

Las Palmas, February 1933. CAP officers stand in front of one of the three Curtiss model 35A Hawk II acquired by the Peruvian government in late 1932. Archive IEHAP.

Lima, a new contract was signed between the Peruvian Government and Faucett airline, this time for a 24-day lease of five aircraft (and their respective crews) to provide transport between San Ramon and Masisea.

The progressive reduction in the number of aircraft available in the different combat units deployed in the east forced V Division Command to take measures to maintain CAP operational capacity in the area. Therefore, by the end April, the surviving Vought O2U-1E Corsair, Douglas O-38P and Curtiss Hawk II were organized within a single unit under the name of *Escuadrón Mixto de Aviación* (Mixed Aviation Squadron, EMA).

On 24 April, the CAP inventory was further reduced when a Fairchild FC-2W flown by Lt. Lapeyre, which was used in transport duties between San Ramón and Masisea, crashed into another aircraft parked by the side of the runway. Fortunately, the pilot came out unscathed after the incident but both aircraft were severely damaged.

Back in Lima, on the afternoon on 30 April at the Santa Beatriz horse racetrack, and as Peruvian President Luis Miguel Sanchez Cerro, aboard his open roof Hispano-Suiza limousine, was conducting a review of EP troops bound to the Putumayo, a young APRA militant disguised as an ice cream man, managed to climb into the car and shot Sanchez Cerro in the chest before being himself

With 2nd Lt. Secada in the cockpit Curtiss Hawk II serial 1/1-VF-1 is ready to depart Puca Barranca forward base bound for another mission. Peruvian Hawk II were delivered in a bright light blue and international orange finish, which made them very hard to conceal in the monochromatic environment of the Amazon forest. Archive IEHAP.

Puca-Barranca, April 1933. A single Hawk II, a trio of O-38P and a Vought Corsair can be seen during a lull in operations at this forward base located on the heart of the Amazon forest.

Puca-Barranca, late March 1933. While ground crews prepare to start the engine of Curtiss serial 1/1-VF-1 a Corsair, identified with serial 5-E-6, is seen starting its take-off run in the background. Archive IEHAP.

killed by the Presidential escort. The death of Sanchez Cerro added yet another crisis to the series of problems faced at the time by the Peruvian Government. Fearing that Sanchez Cerro's death could lead the APRA and the Communist party to incite a popular uprising, and with the objective of maintaining order and government control, the Congress, backed by the military, decided, the very same afternoon of the assassination, to designate General Oscar Raimundo Benavides as interim President for the remaining of Sanchez Cerro's mandate.

In the Putumayo, CAP operations continued apace, and on 4 May another Colombian ship was attacked by Peruvian aircraft, when three Voughts from the EMA (*Escuadrón Mixto de Aviación*) strafed the Colombian transport *Magdalena*, with the Peruvians claiming many Colombian troops killed. Meanwhile, on 5 May, a Fairchild FC-2W and a Ryan B-6 arrived at Las Palmas, both purchased second-hand, once again via H. G. Grow at a unit price of $4,400 and $6,600 US Dollars respectively. These aircraft were sent immediately to San

Hawk II serial 1/1-VF-2 was damaged during landing at Puca-Barranca on April 2, 1933 and could not be repaired before the cease of fire in May. Archive Humberto Currarino.

Itaya 1935, a pilot stands on the starboard float of this Curtiss model 35A Hawk II while ground personnel prepare the aircraft for a routine flight. Archive Humberto Currarino.

2nd Lt. Secada takes off for another escort mission from the waters of the Napo River aboard Hawk II serial 1/1-VF-1. Archive IEHAP.

Aircraft from *IV Escuadrón de Aviación* seen at Cabo Pantoja forward base in late 1935. Located near the Peru-Ecuador border this forward base was of strategic importance for the CAP and units were often deployed there for training. A Curtiss Hawk II, a Hamilton H-45, a single Stearman C-3R and three Curtiss Cyclone Falcon biplanes can be seen in this picture. Archive Roberto Gentili.

Ramón.

The Algodón River Combat

After Colombian public opinion learned of the Peruvian attacks on the vessels *Emmita* and *Sinchi Roca*, as well as other attacks carried out with seeming impunity by the CAP over territory supposedly under Colombian control, the people directed their criticism towards Colonel Boy's capabilities as head of aviation, as well as against General Efraín Rojas, who replaced Vásquez Cobos as head of the Military Expedition, questioning his capabilities to lead the campaign. However, to fully understand the reasons for alleged inaction on the part of Colombian aviation, it is necessary to realize that it did not entirely follow its own command's particular concepts concerning its use – which Rojas intended as a means of attacking only high-value targets such as Puerto Arturo, Güeppi, Iquitos or Leticia itself – but also to numerous other factors of a technical and operational nature, particularly those referring to the employment of the Hawk fighters[27], to which the Colombian Military Aviation (as well as its Peruvian counterpart) was not immune.

Meanwhile, with his pride hurt, and looking to put an end to the CAP's capabilities to fight a war, on 9 May Col. Boy ordered his units stationed across the Putumayo River to remain at constant alert, so that they could react quickly upon the sighting Peruvian intruders.

An aerial view of Keystone serial I-R-7 performing a liaison mission during the first days of January of 1933. Archivo Histórico de la Marina via Gonzalo Maguiña.

A rare view of the only known camouflaged Keystone seen awaiting at the CAP forward base in the Yacu river mouth forward during early February 1932. Archive Humberto Currarino.

A Keystone identified with serial T-057 seen stationed at Puca-Barranca during the autumn of 1933.

Some unidentified CAP officers pose next to a Fairchild FW-2C at San Ramón in the summer of 1933.

After the cease fire of May 1933 the CAP introduced a new series of serials which were used until the summer of 1934. These unidentified men pose along a K-55 identified with the serial T-067, with the T prefix indicating the aircraft function, transport.

This way, the scene was set for the most remarkable air combat of the entire campaign.

The Colombian forces of the *Destacamento Amazonas* were moving towards Puerto Arturo, building a small outpost at Igaraparaná River, while General Rojas also decided to use the vessels of the *Destacamento Putumayo* in the action against the Peruvian town. While the vessels of the *Putumayo* moved towards the mouth of the Campuya River, approaching from the west, the others moved to the Algodón River, on the Peruvian coast of the Putumayo, in two groups, the first with the *Barranquilla*, *Córdova* and *Pichincha* and two launches carrying troops to occupy the place, and the second with the *Mariscal Sucre*, *Bogotá* and *Nariño*. Also, the plan was to threaten Iquitos from the position on the Algodón River, as there were only 200 kilometres between them.

At 2:00 a.m. on 6 May, the first group of vessels passed close to a Peruvian position at Puca-Urco, which was defending the approach to Puerto Arturo. Mines were installed in the river, which were detonated after the *Barranquilla* had passed, while fire was opened from the southern coast. After half an hour, the Colombians retreated and on the following day the Peruvians evacuated that position. After that, the Colombian force reached the mouth of the Algodón River, at about 100 km to the east of Puerto Arturo, and landed.

A single, second hand, Ford AT-4 was purchased by the CAP in early 1933 and pressed into service as heavy transport.

At 0900hrs on 10 May the EMA dispatched a trio of O-38Ps from Puca-Barranca with the mission of patrolling and attacking Colombian river traffic around Puca-Urco, in the Putumayo. As on previous occasions, the CAP relied on the element of surprise as a crucial factor for success, since there were not enough fighters to provide escort to all missions[28]. Nevertheless, confident in their machines and their own capabilities, the crews reached Puca-Urco after almost half an hour of flight. To their surprise, as they were approaching the objective, they observed a flight of three Colombian Hawk II fighters heading towards them. With meagre probabilities of surviving the engagement, the flight leader took the only logical course of action possible and ordered his men to drop their bombs and return to base, diving to gain speed whilst heading back towards Peruvian territory. The Colombian fighters, however, had height advantage and were soon within firing range. In a valorous action, Lt. Americo Vargas, pilot of Douglas serial ½-VG-4, broke formation and lured the Colombian fighters away from the other aircraft, allowing them to escape. In the 3 versus 1 dogfight that ensued, Vargas and his gunner – S.O. Octavio Mendez – and the aircraft were forced to their limits to evade the Colombian fire. As Vargas maneuvered the big biplane as best he could, Mendez made use of his Browning 7.65mm machine gun, managing to keep the Hawks at bay thanks to both the effective defensive fire and evasive manoeuvres – plus the Hawks' lack of manoeuvrability – at least for a while. After several minutes, however, the odds favoured the attackers and the Douglas began to sustain hits which managed to wound both crew members. Realizing

A Travelair S-6000B and a Hamilton H-45 assigned to the *Primer Escuadrón de Transporte Pesado* seen at Cabo Pantoja garrison in early 1935. Archive Roberto Gentili.

that they had run out of luck, Vargas decided to put his aircraft down, landing on the surface of the Algodón River, abandoning the aircraft and taking shelter in the thick jungle. From their hiding spot, they watched the large Douglas, with its floats riddled with bullet holes, as it sank into the river. After avoiding capture by Colombian forces that arrived in the area to recover the aircraft and search for survivors, the valiant aviators were rescued the following day by one of their comrades who arrived in the area aboard a speedboat.

After this incident, the V Division command ordered a halt to all offensive flights over the Putumayo in order to avoid unnecessary losses to the numerically superior Colombian forces.

As there were reports of Peruvian movements towards Tarapacá, the gunboat *Mariscal Sucre*, protected by a pair of Hawks, was sent to explore the Cotuhé River as far as the outpost of Buenos Aires.

Meanwhile, on 22 May, the Colombian F13 serialled 202 was lost in an accident at Caucayá when the crosswind while taking off flipped it and caused it to hit the water almost inverted. The plane was under command of German pilot Schaesberg and Lt. Heriberto Gil, with mechanics Combariza and Fernandez, all of whom died; only the German mechanic Erik Rettich managed to escape from the plane. It was the last loss before the ceasefire.

Chapter 9
CEASEFIRE AND AFTERMATH

During a League of Nations Council extraordinary assembly in Geneva on Wednesday 24 May 1933, the Colombian and Peruvian representatives reached an agreement for the cessation of all military operations in the Putumayo. Likewise, the League ordered the immediate appointment of a Special Commission tasked with the analysis of the legal details of the territorial dispute between both countries, with a final resolution on the subject to be issued within a year.

According to the cease-fire terms, the Peruvian Government agreed to hand over Leticia to the League of Nations' custody and, like the Colombian Government, wait and accept the Commission's final verdict. Colombia, in the meantime, agreed to return all Peruvian territories occupied during the conflict, as well as prisoners of war and equipment captured during the military actions.

The ceasefire put an end to nearly four months of clashes, opening the way to a diplomatic solution of the conflict. Peace between the two countries was finally reached on 19 June 1934, with the signature of the so-called Rio de Janeiro agreement in Brazil.

One of the four Seversky SEV-3M-WW equipped with floats acquired by the Colombian government after the conflict. They performance was very poor because of the floats.

One of the twenty Consolidated PT-11C Husky which arrived in Colombia in 1934 and were serialled 30 to 49.

One of the Colombian PT-11C Husky seen with floats before delivery on 15 July 1934.

Peruvian military aviation rearmament and reorganization

Ironically, despite the fact that Peruvian military aviation started the campaign in better – although not ideal – condition than its Colombian counterpart, the CAP's weaknesses in training and organization began to manifest throughout the campaign in the form of accidents and these, not Colombian fire, were the major cause of losses – between September 1932 and March 1933 – of 60 % of the total CAP strength in the theatre of operations.

Given the lack of funding for combat aviation, and as the amount raised by the *Colecta Nacional* proved insufficient to fulfil the Armed

A Bellanca model 77-140 acquired by Colombia to act as light bomber.

A poor quality picture of FAC 621, but on which the ventral gunner position is clearly visible. Archive Santiago Rivas.

The Bellanca model 77-140 was unequivocally the ugly duck which never turned into a swan. This big, ugly and unorthodox design saw limited use with Colombian military aviation. Archive Dan Hagedorn.

A PT-11C acquired by the Colombian government seen shortly after rolling out from the Consolidated assembly line in Buffalo, New York. These aircraft could be equipped with conventional landing gear as well as with floats. Archive Dan Hagedorn.

One of the three Curtis BT-32 Condor purchased by Colombia after the conflict, to act as transports and medium bombers.

The Colombian Curtiss Condors and the first three Junkers Ju52/3m could be used both as transports and bombers.

Forces' requirements, the Peruvian Government, via the special economic budged initiative called "expenses for the national defence" (authorized by Supreme Decrees N°7595 and N°7597) allowed the external indebtedness of the country to increase with the purpose of financing the necessary material for national defence. The CAP, after failing to obtain additional sources of modern aircraft in the US, turned to Europe to satisfy its requirements, dispatched technical commissions to France, Italy, Germany and the United Kingdom to evaluate the suitability of the material offered by each of these countries' manufacturers, and ascertain whether or not they complied with the CAP technical requirements. This process ended with the signature of the following contracts:

1. Société Générale Aéronautique. A pair of contracts were signed on the 16 and 18 of February of 1933 for the purchase of the following aircraft:

- Six Hanriot H.438[29], at a unit price of 270,000 Francs,
- Six Morane Saulnier Ms.316ET2, at a unit price of 162,000 Francs,
- A single Morane Saulnier M.S.231ET[30], at a unit price of 180,000 Francs,
- Twelve Potez 390A.2[31], at a unit price of 588,000 Francs and,
- Twelve Nieuport Delage NiD.121C.1[32], at a unit price of 505, 000 Francs.

2. Chance-Vought Aircraft Corporation. A contract was signed on 4 April 1933, for the purchase of:

- Three O2U-3B Corsair, at a unit price of $30,500 US Dollars,
- Three Vought V-80P, at a unit price of $29,800 US Dollars.

3. Fairey Aviation Company Limited. A contract signed on 12 April 1933, for the purchase of:

Side view of a Colombian Curtiss Condor, where the defensive positions on the back of the plane are clearly visible, as well as on top of the fuselage, behind the cockpit.

Interestingly, this Colombian Condor has the floats camouflaged, while the plane is painted on silver.

A Colombian Curtiss Condor seen before delivery.

Three of the four Bellanca model 77-140 light bombers purchased by Colombia and received after the conflict.

One of the first three Junkers Ju52/3m at Girardot. They considerably increased the transport and attack capabilities of the Colombian Military Aviation.

Three of the four Colombian Seversky SEV-3M-WW seen before delivery.

The first of the three Colombian Curtiss Condors, with serial 651.

One of the three Curtiss Condors delivered to the Colombian Military Aviation, seen before delivery.

One of the Colombian Curtiss Condor before delivery.

A Bellanca Air Bomber 77-140 for the Colombian Military Aviation being assembled.

The three Colombian Curtiss Condors flying in formation shortly after their arrival. Photo Gumersindo Cuellar.

The Junkers Ju52/3m serialled 623, the third from the initial batch of the model purchased by the Colombian Military Aviation. The order was made through SCADTA.

Curtiss Condors with floats and Junkers Ju52/3m on wheels seen at Palanquero shortly after the conflict.

A Curtiss Condor of the Colombian Military Aviation operating at Palanquero.

Ford 5-AT-89 Tri Motor at North Beach, New York, before being delivered to Colombia. Note the name "Shell" deleted from the fuselage, as the plane belonged to that oil company previously.

FAC 621 at SCADTA's airport in Barranquilla. Note the ventral position for the gunner visible. Archive Santiago Rivas.

The CAP also received a batch of six Morane Saulnier Ms.316 primary trainers. This model was a development of the MS.301 fitted with a 100hp Lorraine 5P engine. Archive Michael Liebert.

One of the four Ford 5-AT Tri Motor purchased by the Colombian Military Aviation for use as transports.

The FAC 621 on the Magdalena River. Note the doors on the right side, the windshield of the early Ju52/3m and the ventral gunner position. Archive Santiago Rivas.

In 1934 the CAP issued an order for a batch of the elegant Nieuport-Delage 121C.1 parasol fighter, by the time still in the prototype stage. Only thirteen units of this type were produced and twelve of them saw service with the CAP. Archive Michel Liebert.

Las Palmas, June 1933. Line-up of Hanriot H.438 and Morane Saulnier MS.316 trainers shortly after delivery. Archive Humberto Currarino.

CAP took delivery of six Hanriot H.438 conversion biplanes in the summer of 1933. These aircraft were a variant of the H.433 re-engined with a 240hp Lorraine 7M Mizar engine. Archive Michel Liebert.

The need for advanced trainers lead the CAP to focus in the procurement of substantial numbers of instruction aircraft. The Morane Saulnier Ms.231E.2 advanced trainer was one of the several aircraft of its category acquired during the aftermath of the conflict. Archive Humberto Currarino.

Having an all metal, or mostly metallic structure was a requisite established by the technical evaluation committee during the Peruvian acquisitions of 1933 and 1934. The Potez 390A.2, of which twelve were ordered by the CAP, accomplished those requisites. Archive José Fernández.

- Six Fairey Seal observation and attack aircraft, for a total amount of 1,303,000 Soles de Oro,
- Six Fairey Fox IV, for a similar amount.

4. Societa Aeroplani Caproni S.p.A.. A contract was signed on 10April 1934, allowed the acquisition of:

- Twelve Caproni Ca.111, and
- Twelve Caproni Ca.114, for an approximate total of 14,700,000 Italian Lire.

5. Curtiss-Wright Export Company. On 12 May 1934, a final contract was signed with the Curtiss-Wright Export Co. for:

- Ten Curtiss model 37F Cyclone Falcon observation and light attack biplanes, at a unit price of $28,500 US Dollars, as well as
- Four Curtiss Model 35A Hawk II[33], at a unit price of $25,000 US Dollars.

It is worth noting that, in most cases, the large amounts paid for each aircraft were caused by the inclusion of interchangeable landing gear/float sets for each aircraft, as well as other modifications requested by the CAP in accordance to the requirements of the CTA.

A Potez 390A.2 of the *Cuarta Escuadrilla de Observación* (Fourth *Observation Escadrille*) at Las Palmas on early 1935.

The CAP ordered a dozen of the Ca.114 biplane fighter, a competitor to the FIAT Cr.32 during the 1933-34 *Regia Aeronautica´s* rearming process. As with other aircraft acquired in the immediate cease-fire period this fighter could be fitted with floats if required for operations in the Amazon rivers.

A line-up of aircraft composed by at least nine Potez 390A.2 seen at Las Palmas in late 1934. Archive Michel Ledet.

A formation of CAP Hanriots over Lima. Archive Javier Goto.

Regia Aeronautica Lieutenant Luigi Bianchi was one of the two officers sent to Perú to train the CAP officers in the use of their new mounts. Bianchi remained in the South American country until mid-1937 when he returned to Italy. Archive Roberto Gentili.

When fitted with the 720hp Lorraine Petrel Hars 12-cylinder 720hp engine the NiD.123C.1 was born. Archive Michel Ledet.

Demonstrations made to the CAP Delegation by Italian Lt. Bianchi with the Caproni Ca.111 Idro.

Although the aircraft comprising this list represented – at least on paper – an impressive air fleet, equal to or, in some cases, exceeding in quality and quantity the aircraft purchased by Colombia, the fact remains that most of these were still to be delivered after a long journey from Europe or, even worse, some of them still had to be manufactured, meaning that Peruvian aviation would have to continue fighting in conditions of numerical inferiority up until 24 May, when the League of Nations' peace formula was accepted by both parties, opening the road for twelve months of "armed peace". The CAP used this window of opportunity to repair aircraft damaged during the combat actions, to receive and assimilate most of the recently purchased material and, more importantly, to give the aircrews a most welcomed rest. Finally, this time period also served for the CAP High Command to evaluate their combat crews' performance, weaknesses and strengths during the campaign.

Meanwhile, at the time of the cease-fire, MGP units began their deployment to the Pacific Coast of Colombia, via the Panama Canal and then into the Amazon River, in what could be considered as a risky gamble. Such units would have had to operate without any kind of air support whatsoever, other than a lone Vought UO-1A which was embarked aboard BAP *Grau* and was insufficient to provide appropriate air cover to the naval units. Had hostilities continued, the

Dissasembled Ca.111 airframes await their turn to be loaded into the freighter that will transport them from the Italian port of Genoa to Callao, in Lima. Caproni Museum via Giorgio Apostolo.

Three of the planes sent to Peru arrived ready for action, as was required by the CAP. In the picture, one of them is being put into the water at Callao harbour in Lima. Caproni Museum via Giorgio Apostolo.

As was the case with other manufacturers, Nieuport-Delage also adapted floats to its NiD-121 fighter in order to fulfil the CAP requirements. Archive Michel Liebert.

MGP would most certainly have suffered the loss of their naval units to Colombian aviation, evidencing – early as these times were in the history of modern warfare – the decline of naval power in favour of combat aviation.

Finally, it can be concluded that improvisation, lack of training and poor operational conditions were to blame for the disastrous campaign results for the CAP, which suffered the loss of 11 aircraft during nine months of operations. On the other hand, Colombia registered the loss of four aircraft in diverse accidents, mostly due to mechanical causes. However, the lessons left by that campaign were of vital importance for CAP High Command and resulted in better and more efficient acquisition, training and logistics control procedures, marking the beginning of a remarkable improvement in its capabilities. As consequence, only a year and a half after the end of the Putumayo campaign under difficult material conditions, the CAP became one of the main air powers in Latin America, thanks to both the quality and quantity of its equipment, as well as the training and organization.

Ancón, by the end of 1934. This picture shows the movement of a Ca.111 from its hangar to the sea before a routine mission from the facilities of the *III Escuadrón de Aviación*. Archive IEHAP.

Three Ca.100S.63 basic trainers and one Caproni Ca.113 for advanced training and aerobatics arrived in Peru in 1934. Archive John Davis.

A line of Six Fairey Seal, a Ryan B-6, the single Consolidated PT-3 Husky, a Curtiss C-3R and one of the Curtiss Fledgling seen parked at Las Palmas in the summer of 1933.

A Fairey Seal from the 1st Bombardment and Observation Squadron assigned under the command of the *III EA* suffered damaged to its lower rear section and was sent to Las Palmas for repairs. IEHAP Archive.

Taken in early 1934 at Las Palmas, two Fox IV together with three Curtiss Model 37F Cyclone Falcon, three Curtiss model 35A Hawk II and other planes. Archive Humberto Currarino.

The elegant Fairey Fox was another of the types acquired in June 1934 with the aim to rearm the CAP for a protracted conflict in June of 1934.

Ancon, July 1934. With the arrival of new aircraft several new units were organized. This image shows an old UO-1A from 2da Escuadrilla de Instrucción and a recently arrived Fairey Seal from the newly activated 2do Escuadrón de Observacion. Archivo Histórico de la Marina.

Colombian purchases

The Colombian government also continued to reinforce their military aviation, while the material bought by the end of 1932 continued arriving during 1933. Also, the base at Palanquero was expanded considerably, with two large hangars in addition to the hangar already in existence, and inaugurated on 17 October 1933 as *Base Central*. This base became the most important one for the Colombian Military Aviation, operating almost all planes, except for those at the *Escuela de Aviación Militar*, moved to Cali in 1933. Also, in 1934 the *Base Aérea de San José del Guaviare* was inaugurated near the city of Villavicencio, about 70 kilometers to the southeast of Bogotá, on the lower plains at the foot of the Andes.

In 1933 the school received five Curtiss Wright CW-16, serialled 21 to 26; twenty Consolidated PT-11C Husky arrived in 1934 and were serialled 30 to 49, along with five Fairchild 22-C7F with serials 51 to 55, being the backbone of the aviation training until World War 2. To reinforce the transport fleet of Junkers Ju52/3m, four Ford 5-AT-C Tri motors and three Curtis BT-32 Condor were purchased, all equipped with wheels or floats. The Condors arrived in 1934 and received serials 651 to 653, and the Fords in 1935, having serials 641 to 644.

The combat aviation was slightly improved, with the purchase of four Bellanca Air Bomber 77-140 light bombers, based on the Bellanca Air Cruiser, which arrived in 1935 in Palanquero and received serials 671 to 674. As fighters, four Seversky SEV-3M-WW equipped with floats were serialled 180 to 183, but their performance was poor – due to the resistance caused by the floats – and were retired in 1946, while the Curtiss Hawks remained as the main fighter of the force until replaced by the Republic P-47D Thunderbolts in 1946.

Flight line at Las Palmas on November 1933. Three Fairey Fox IV can be seen together with five Fairey Seal together with other planes acquired during the year. Alarco family archive.

Officers of the *2do Escuadron de Observación* with one of the Seals of the unit who operated from Ancón. Archivo Histórico de la Marina.

NOTES

1 Panama returned to Colombia and in 1903 became independent again.
2 Named after the men who signed it: Alberto Salomón, Peruvian Foreign Relations minister, and Mr. Fabio Lozano T., Colombian representative in Lima.
3 Basadre, *Problema y sociedad y otros ensayos*, Lima, 1965; p.12
4 *Documentos sobre la Campaña del Nor Oriente*, CEHM, Legajo No.2; p.14.
5 RESEÑA HISTORICA BASE ARSENAL MADRID. Parte 1, 1924-1933. p.270
6 RESEÑA HISTORICA BASE ARSENAL MADRID. Parte 1, 1924-1933. pp.274-276
7 Hagedorn, *Latin American Air Wars*, 2006, Chapter 4; p.4
8 Both the K43 and the W34 purchased via SCADTA. The K43 were had constructor numbers 2571 to 2573 and serials 57, 58 and 59, later changed to correlative serials 401 to 403, respectively. The W34 had constructor numbers 2823, 2824, 2826, 2831, 2833 and 2834, receiving serials 404 to 409. These aircraft were powered by BMW-licensed built Pratt & Whitney T1D1 Hornet engines.
9 The first three units, identified with constructor numbers 4010 to 4012 and Colombian Military serials 621 to 623, were diverted from an order made by SCADTA in April 1933 while the remaining units arrived from Germany on 5 July 1933, and assigned with the correlative serials 624 to 626. All these aircraft were fitted with Pratt & Whitney T1D1 Hornet engines.
10 Purchased in Germany via SCADTA and identified with Co/No 221/34 and Co/No 222/35, with AM serials 603 and 604. These Napier Lion engine machines arrived on 12.01.32 aboard S.S. *Heinz Horn*, which also brought along some German "volunteers" and joined in operations the ex-SCADTA Dornier J serials AM 601 and AM 602 already in service with the Colombians.
11 Six of which were delivered between October 31, 1932 and January 9, 1933, receiving AM serials 801 to 805 (with one aircraft apparently left unserialed).
12 Identified with AM serials 610 and 611. The first of these machines was delivered on January 1933. Hagedorn, Latin American Air Wars; p.10
13 20 units were ordered in 1932 with nine being delivered in Colombia between March and May, 1933 and assigned with correlative serials AM 111 to AM 130. In 1934 five additional units were ordered as replacement for operational losses and assigned with the serials AM 111-A, 115-A, 116-A, 118-A and the AM 131.
14 An ad-hoc outfit composed by members from the three branches of the armed forces.
15 The 640hp Wright R-1820F "Cyclone" radial engine.
16 *Conflict Amazónico 1932/1934*, General Álvaro Valencia Tovar, Villegas Editores, Bogotá, 1994.
17 *Armed forces of Latin America*, Adrian English, Jane's Publishing Company, London, 1984.
18 *Conflicto Amazónico*, 1932 – 1934, Álvaro Valencia Tovar, Villegas Editores, Bogotá, 1994.
19 Which served as headquarters for V Division high command. *Documentos sobre la campaña Perú-Colombia*, legajo 2; p.60.
20 The son of infamous Cauchero Julio C. Arana. Arana's presence in Puerto Arturo can be interpreted as evidence of the interests hiding behind the actions of September 1st.
21 *Télégraphie sans fil.*
22 Radiogram issued by Joint Forces C-in-C in Iquitos to the MMA in Lima from December 14, 1932. *Documentos sobre la campaña Perú-Colombia*. Legajo 2, CEHM, p.60.
23 Peruvian Steamship Co.
24 *Una historia con Alas,* Herbert Boy, edited by the Fuerza Aérea Colombiana, Bogotá, Colombia, 2009.
25 Wright 1820-F engines ran on 87 octane fuel, which was practically nonexistent at the front at that time, so the lower 84 octane fuel was employed instead.
26 Aboard his Corsair was gold and money sent from the capital and required to the war effort. The aircraft, along with the crew remains, were only found eleven years later, in 1944.
27 These, like Peruvian machines, did not have electric starters and, therefore, they had to be started by ground crews manually with the inherent prejudice in the response time.
28 The Hawk serial 1/1-VF-1 was the only CAP fighter left in the theater after 1/1-VF-2 was damaged in an incident in April and was undergoing repairs at the time. On May 10 this aircraft was flown on a search mission for the Hamilton 1-R-10.
29 Essentially a Hanriot 431 powered by a 240hp Lorraine Mizar 7M engine.
30 M.S.230 variant, powered by the same 240hp Lorraine engine as the Hanriot 438.
31 Powered by a 550 hp Lorraine Petrel Hars engine. Although the official Potez nomenclature for this variant was type 390, Peruvian machines wore the Potez 39A.2 denomination the tail, a common French aircraft manufacturer's tradition, meaning perhaps that the factory employed already built airframes fitted with the new engines.
32 Original order was composed by ten NiD.121C1 and three NiD.626C1. Long delays in the delivery schedule of the later, however, caused the Peruvian MG to cancel the NiD.626 order, replacing them by two additional samples of the more modern 121C.1.
33 Both powered by 640hp Wright R-1820-F Cyclone engines.

BIBLIOGRAPHY

Abate, R., *Gli Aeroplani della Caproni Bergamasca 1920-1946*, Milan: Dell' Ateneo & Bizzari, 1978.

Andersson, Lennart, Günter Endres, Günther Ott, Rob Mulder, *Junkers F13, the world's first all-metal airliner*, N.p. (UK): EAM Books, 2012.

Arias de Greiff, Gustavo, *Decolando contra el viento, 100 años de la aviación en Colombia*, Bogotá: Villegas Editores, Bogotá, 2013.

Aviación, magazine of the Cuerpo Aeronáutico Peruano, Dirección de Información CAP, Lima: Imprenta CAP, 1936-40.

Boy, Herbert, Fuerza Aérea Colombiana (ed.), *Una historia con Alas*, Bogotá: Fuerza Aérea Colombiana, Colombia, 2009.

von Buddenbrock, Fr. Frhr., *Atlantico-Pacifico, Lehrjahre des überseeischen Luftverkehrs*, Düsseldorf: GFW Verlag, 1965.

Burden, William A.M., *The struggle for airways in Latin America*, Washington D.C.: Council on Foreign Relations, 1943.

Ciccarelli, Orazio, 'Fascism and Politics in Peru during the Benavides Regime, 1933-39: The Italian Perspective' in: *Hispanic American Historical Review*, Vol 70, No.3, August 1990, pp.405-432.

Del Caproni al MiG-29: Páginas de Oro de *la Base Aérea de Chiclayo, Grupo Aéreo Nº6*, Chiclayo: Editorial Aquije, 2005.

English, Adrian, *Armed Forces of Latin America*, London: Jane's Publishing Company, London, 1984.

Forero, Coronel José Ignacio, *Historia de la Aviación en Colombia*, Bogotá: Aedita Editores, 1964.

Fuerza Aérea Colombiana (ed.), *Fuerza Aérea Colombiana, Su epopeya y su grandeza, 1919-1974*, Bogotá: Fuerza Aérea Colombiana, 1974.

Gentilli, Roberto, *L'Aviazione Da Caccia Italiana, 1918-1939, Volume II: Tecnica, Stemmi, Esportazioni,* Firenze: Ed.A.I., 1982.

Hagedorn, Dan, *Latin American Air Wars and Aircraft*, Mardens Hill: Hikoki Publications, 2006.

Instruzioni per il montamento e per la regolazione dell`Aeroplano Caproni 111 IIª serie: Direzione Generale delle Contruzione e degli Approvvigionamenti, Roma: Ministero dell'Aeronautica, 1935.

Instruzioni per il montamento e per la regolazione dell`Aeroplano Caproni 113: Direzione Generale delle Contruzione e degli Approvvigionamenti, Roma: Ministero dell'Aeronautica, 1935.

Legislación Naval y Aeronáutica, Tomo XI, Lima, 1937.

Racines, Mayor (R) Oscar Forero, Fuerza Aérea Colombiana (ed.), *Fuerza Aérea Colombiana, 75 años en los cielos patrios*, Bogotá: Fuerza Aérea Colombiana, 1994.

Ramírez Alfaro, Luis, *Historia Aeronáutica del Perú* (Volume IX), Lima: Imprenta FAP, 1986.

Regolazione Tecnica e Norme de Montaggio e Regolazione dell `Aeroplano Caproni 114 di Difesa Motore Mercurio: Direzione Generale delle Contruzione e degli Approvvigionamenti, Roma: Ministero dell'Aeronautica, 1935.

Regolazione Tecnica e Norme de Montaggio e Regolazione dell `Aeroplano Caproni 135 "Perú", Direzione Generale delle Contruzione e degli Approvvigionamenti, Roma: Ministero dell'Aeronautica, 1938.

Scheina, Robert, *Latin America's Wars*, Washington DC: Brassey's, 2003.

Tincopa, Amaru & Santiago Rivas, *Axis Aircraft in Latin America*, Manchester: Hikoki, 2016.

Tovar, Álvaro Valencia, *Conflicto Amazónico, 1932–1934*, Bogotá: Villegas Editores, 1994.

Valdez Arroyo, Flor de María, *Las Relaciones entre Perú e Italia (1821-2002)*, Lima: Instituto de Estudios Internacionales, Pontificia Universidad Católica del Perú, 2004.

van der Mey, M. Michel, *Dornier Wal, A light coming over the sea*, Trento, Italy: LoGisma Editore, 2005.

Zlatar Stambuk, José, *César Alvares Guerra*, Lima: FAP Press, 2005.

ACKNOWLEDGEMENTS

The authors wish to thank Javier Franco, Mauricio Umaña, Rafael González Richmond, and the Colombian Air Force Museum for their help.

ABOUT THE AUTHORS

Amaru Tincopa was born in Lima, Perú in 1977. A graduate in Law, he developed a strong taste for history from a very young age which this lead to researching articles and books about Peruvian and Latin American military aviation history.

He published his first book in 2003, dealing with the history of the Aeroplani Caproni aircraft and industrial endeavour in Perú for an Italian editorial. Another 10 titles have followed since then in Argentina, France and the United Kingdom, with three more in the pipeline.

He currently collaborates with several renowned magazines specialising in military aviation history across the world.

Santiago Rivas was born in Buenos Aires, Argentina in 1977. Twenty years later, the Journalism graduate started to work in the fields of aviation and defence journalism – travelling all across Latin America to conduct his research for articles and books.

In 2007 he published his first book, which was about the Malvinas/Falklands War, for a Brazilian editor – and since then another 12 have been published across the globe in Argentina, Brazil, France, Germany and the United Kingdom, while four more are soon to be released. He has also had articles published in more than 50 magazines in 20 countries – and he currently works for more than 20 of the magazines.

Santiago has three children and lives in Buenos Aires. He continues to travel every year to most of the Latin American countries to fulfil his research-based work.